Film and
Television Acting

Film and Television Acting

Ian Bernard

Focal Press
Boston   London

Focal Press is an imprint of Butterworth-Heinemann.

Copyright © 1993 by Butterworth-Heinemann, a division of Reed Publishing (USA) Inc.
All rights reserved.

An excerpt from CHEERS courtesy of Paramount Pictures.

Library of Congress Cataloging-in-Publication Data
Bernard, Ian (Ian J.), 1930–
    Film and television acting / Ian Bernard.
        p.   cm.
    Includes index.
    ISBN 0-240-80138-5 (alk. paper)
    1. Motion picture acting.   2. Acting for television.   I. Title.
    PN1995.9.A26B47   1993
    791.43'028–dc20   92-23281
                                                                            CIP

British Library Cataloguing-in-Publication Data
A catalogue record for this book is available from the British Library.

Butterworth-Heinemann
80 Montvale Avenue
Stoneham, MA 02180

10 9 8 7 6 5 4 3 2 1

Printed in the United States of America

□ □ □
□ □ □
□ □ □

Contents

□ □ □
□ □ □
□ □ □

Preface

Dame Judith Anderson, the Australian actress, began her career on stage. When she did her first movie, she tells this story. "When I finished a scene, the director called me over and whispered, 'Watch your eyebrows.' I asked him what he meant and he went on to explain that when you raise your eyebrows on stage it was a matter of an inch, but when you raised them in a close up on the movie screen, it was three feet."

In that one inch to three foot equation lies a fundamental difference between stage acting and acting for TV and movies. Modern stage acting has become more naturalistic, and, in a way, more cinematic. Even so, in acting for film and television, there are moments, whether in preparation or performance, where the actor should be aware of what the camera and microphone can do. The barely audible sigh on stage can be detected by the audience as a rising of the chest. In film, the sigh is heard and, for emphasis, can be made louder. When one knows how these things are done, this awareness, when properly applied, allows the actor to develop techniques especially for the camera.

Film and Television Acting examines these techniques in detail. No matter what experience, acting method, or training, the actor will be able to correlate the ideas in this book to what they already know about the craft.

One last note: All exercises in the book must be video taped, utilizing the close up shot as much as possible. A VCR and monitor are also necessary.

Acknowledgments

I would like to thank the following people who consented to be interviewed especially for this book.

Norman Jewison: Producer/Director. Some of his credits include, *In the Heat of the Night*, *The Russians are Coming*, and *Moonstruck*.

Glenn Jordan: Producer/Director. Mr. Jordan began as a theater director. He's won five Emmys for television directing ("Promise," starring James Wood and James Garner was one of them), and has also directed three feature films.

Louise Latham: Character actress. Ms. Latham has had a long career on stage and film. Her most recent stage role was in Sam Shepard's *Lies of the Mind*. One of her memorable films was Hitchcock's *Marnie*.

Jack Lemmon: Mr. Lemmon has won two Academy Awards: best supporting actor for *Mr. Roberts*, and best actor in *Save the Tiger*. His most recent stage appearances include *Tribute* and *The Iceman Cometh*.

Don Murray: Actor/Producer/Director. Mr. Murray began as a stage actor. His films include, *Bus Stop* and *Hoodlum Priest*, plus several TV movies. He also had a continuing role in "Knott's Landing."

□ □ □
□ □ □
□ □ □

Foreword

by Jack Lemmon

There are many books on the technique of acting and rightly so. Acting is a rich, diverse art that invites analysis, experiment, and criticism. Until now there hasn't been a book that examines the particular differences between stage, film, and television. That is why I am so pleased to write the foreword for this book.

Film and Television Acting methodically examines the techniques of acting for camera and shows how they differ from stage acting. True, many of the techniques are alike and some of the differences are minuscule. But these subtle variations can be quite obvious when blown up on the screen. Between doing too much and too little, there is a subtle area where things feel just right. This book gives the actor definitive techniques to discover that place.

It doesn't matter what basic acting technique you use. Ian Bernard's methods are ones of modification and enhancement, rather than change. The three elements in the book—interviews, exercises, and instruction—combine to give a complete and thorough analysis of what actors should do in front of the camera. The book also takes a realistic look at the work place and tells you what to expect on the set.

My first film was called, *It Should Happen to You*, and I was fortunate enough to play the lead opposite Judy Holliday. The director was the great George Cukor, one of the very finest directors for actors. In the beginning, after almost every take he would say, "Wonderful, just wonderful, but let's do it once more. Jack . . . give me less."

This went on for days, me acting my head off and George saying, "Less, Jack. Less."

Finally, in complete frustration, I turned to him and said, "Are you trying to tell me not to act?"

"Oh God, yes!" he quickly replied.

When you read this book, you'll know what George Cukor meant.

I believe the actor has to learn to "trust the camera." *Film and Television Acting* teaches one how to gain that trust in a logical and direct manner.

1

□ □ □
□ □ □
□ □ □

The Evolving Play Vs. the Frozen Film

Although they might deny it, actors appearing in long running plays perform by rote at times. Rex Harrison once confessed that during the run of *My Fair Lady* there were times in the second act when he wondered what he was going to have for supper after the performance. The intrinsic nature of a stage play creates an atmosphere wherein a variety of things can happen in performance depending on the reaction of the audience. The actors often say, "It was a good audience tonight," when everything seemed to click.

I have never heard a stage actor say, "It was a good performance because our rehearsal period and preparation made it possible." Now you realize the rehearsal preparation was done weeks before, so theoretically, everything had been set. All the questions about interpretation should have been answered. Night after night the actors perform the same words, the same actions. But, even though the actor does the same ritualistic tune-ups before going on each time, each performance is different. It is this feeling that attracts so many actors to stage acting: that no matter how planned everything is, each performance is new. There is nothing like the immediate response from a live audience.

The variety of this response at any performance depends on a lot of factors. For one thing, if the actors are good enough technically, the audience's reception will always be positive, even if the performances from the actors' point of view were just so-so.

This sense of creative discovery in each performance doesn't exist for the actor in film, though. She must be prepared to create a part and know that as soon as it is filmed, her performance will never change. Except for Woody Allen, I know of no filmmakers who, after viewing the scenes, are allowed to reshoot until they are satisfied. The usual procedure is to shoot as many takes of the scene as needed. Then, the director decides to move on. But once that decision is made, there's no turning back. To redo a scene days or weeks later is rare, and is more often caused by the film being damaged at the lab than by

1

a director wishing to reshoot. This means one thing to the actor: You have one chance to get it right.

> *The essential thing is to determine who the character is and the choices you make in relation to this character and this particular material. You study the material pretty much the same way in stage or film, but then it is more a technique of delivering the character in front of the camera. Lawrence Olivier was talking about character work and said: "I think in the theatre you can inhabit a character, but in film, the character must inhabit you.*
>
> Louise Latham

OK, so Olivier said the character must inhabit you. But Jack Lemmon said: "I'm not as interested in how a character should behave as how he *could* behave. If I can legitimately find a way that's very exciting, then I'll push to do that." So, the idea is to find the character and then perhaps go one step further? In film and television, this is disastrous. A little bit of ham on stage becomes a feast on camera.

Most actors have no problem with going one step further. It's called overacting. But there's a greater problem with the actor who never allows that to happen. The fear of doing too much has led to some pretty dull performances. The trick is to find the correct, most comfortable and honest place. One of the best ways of doing that is to listen and react, listen and react.

The actor on stage has two reactive elements to deal with—the other actors and the audience. Because each actor senses audience reactions and each, in his own way, behaves differently because of that, the play is ever-changing from moment to moment. The film actor has no such feedback. When the scene is over, the director may offer suggestions to modify the performance, but while the scene is being filmed, the actors are on their own.

The expression goes, "The director asked for a closeup, and there was nobody home." It means the actor's eyes were vacant—not a thought could be seen.

How do you keep somebody home?

2

□ □ □
□ □ □
□ □ □

Listening and Reacting

I can't prove it, but I would surmise that every teenager in the world has at one time complained, "Nobody ever listens to me." Experts are hired by large, important corporations to give seminars on how to listen. It is quite probable there would be no more war if people listened to one another. Listening is the vital first link in communication, and since acting is an artistic form of communicating, one would think that actors were superb listeners. They're not.

The Reaction Shot

We all know you can do a lot without saying anything in behavior. . . . You can do more with one eyebrow sometimes, then with ten lines of dialogue. If you can do it with a look, it might be better.

Robert De Niro

In the movies and television there is something called the *reaction shot.* That is a close shot where one actor is listening to another actor and reacts to what is being said. (There is no such animal in the theatre.) The reaction shot is often used to reinforce the way the director wants the audience to respond. The actor listens and reacts. The audience empathizes and does likewise. In the process of editing the reaction shot is used to cover up a technical glitch or a bad performance from the other actor. It is also used in the editing process to create a dramatic pause and for comic timing. Successful pacing of a movie depends on the editor having a choice of different shots. For example, in the first shooting of a scene, the shot encompasses both actors. (This is the master shot.) Then the scene is repeated with only actor one and then again with actor two alone in the shot. There are now three versions of the scene. With their choice of which shots to use, the director and editor can control the timing. They can also cut away from the speaking actor to the listening actor, thus controlling dramatic emphasis as well.

The reaction shot is one of the most important elements of film acting. It's

3

usually done in closeup or over the speaking actor's shoulder right after the director has shot the master. You, the listening actor, may or may not have lines to speak. The important thing is to hear the words spoken to you and make the viewer believe you have never heard them before.

One often hears a director say, "Keep alive!" which loosely translated means, "Think! Keep thinking!" In preparing a stage role, the actor does her homework by making character bios, plotting and analyzing scenes, and doing whatever else it takes to play the part. She reacts according to the material and to the other characters. The film and television actor usually performs the same process but then should take it a step further.

The actor never knows when those closeups will occur. He could be called on at any time for a reaction shot. Let's say, for instance, the actor who is speaking is going on about a school he went to back in Ohio. Along with other facts, the reacting actor loves the character who's speaking. The speech is 10 seconds long. By the way, this is a very long time on screen. Does the reacting actor play ten seconds of love?

That one emotion may be enough, but then, it may not. Since the actor doesn't know prior to shooting when these reaction shots may happen, he must prepare in a general way. It is then that the subtleties of film acting come into play.

The stage actor may prepare a subtext with one idea, one objective, and that usually suffices. But the film actor has the opportunity to take a certain moment and play a variety of emotions. (Of course they must be appropriate to the scene.) It is possible then for the editor to use this one closeup in other scenes if needed. In other words, if the actor plays a variety of emotions, the shot can be used in a variety of places. Editors sometimes steal a shot from one scene and put it someplace else in the movie. (That is, providing locale and costume are the same.) Of course, the actor must be careful not to overdo the variety of emotions. Time and time again the actor must remember that what seems normal for the stage will appear too much for the camera. It's best to keep the emotions in a related channel, that is with love, the actor's thought might be of the first kiss, our special place, marriage, honeymoon, children, and so on.

The reaction shot, to be effective, depends wholly on the ability of the actor to listen!

Listening

It's fatal to act in film. Listening is the most important thing. Think about what is being said.

Rex Harrison

The actor on stage stands with head cocked to one side. The face is intent. The body is tense. All of the signs point to one person listening to another. The audience believes he's listening. The director at the back of the house believes it. Even the other actor in the scene believes it. Yet it is possible for the listening actor to fool everyone at that moment. And, like Rex Harrison when he wondered about supper during a performance, the actor's mind can wander off, he can lose focus (it doesn't matter what you call it) and not be able to get back. At one time or another, every actor has done it.

Most of the time, the actor clicks in, and no one except the actor is the wiser. The expressions "going up," "drawing a blank," "losing your place," all refer to this lapse of focus.

The going up process begins with the conscious knowledge the listening actor has of the other actor's lines. They are no longer words but cues. The listener has heard them in rehearsal and at each performance. The words lose their meaning and the actor no longer listens to them—only pretends to. Pretending to listen can work on stage, but never in film or television.

Listening doesn't merely mean you're supposed to look at someone and listen to the words. It is listening to the real intent behind what the hell they're doing. No man did that better than Spencer Tracy. He could hold you for five minutes while somebody else was talking . . . . He may be looking around, looking at the floor, but you could tell something was going on in his mind. The problem for an actor is to reach the point where he trusts himself to just think. I still, and always will, find it difficult at times to trust myself. It is seldom that I think I've been guilty of underacting. When I'm wrong, or off, it will usually be because I've done too much.

Jack Lemmon

There is a story about Marlon Brando when he made a picture called *The Freshman*. Brando purposely didn't learn his lines. Instead, he had a small speaker put in his ear so that when it was his turn to speak, someone told him his line via the speaker, and then Brando delivered it in person. The reason for this, the story goes, was that Brando wanted to be sure that each line was fresh, and the time he spent listening to his line before speaking it would assure that the timing was correct.

Since most other actors, no, make that *all* other actors, will never have that kind of treatment, it is necessary to discover a technique to achieve the same results.

Spencer Tracy was reported to have said, "Know your lines, show up on time, and don't bump into the furniture." Mr. Tracy had the ability to know his lines in such a way that the audience had the impression he had just thought of them a moment before speaking. I've heard a few actors say they purposely don't memorize the lines to keep them fresh. I think this is an excuse for laziness and poor technique. Because of that, they end up paraphrasing, which I will write more of later.

Knowing your lines gives you the freedom to listen and react in an honest, emotional way.

EXERCISE 1: LISTENING

The camera is close up on the listening actor. The questioning actor (off camera but very close to it) waits for an answer, then goes to the next question. The two actors should have eye contact, and at no time should the actor on camera look into the lens.

Questions

These are sample questions, but you may substitute questions of your own. In fact, it is better to have fresh questions for each actor if the exercise is done in a group.

1. How old are you?
2. Where is Mount Everest?
3. Where were you two years ago?
4. What is your favorite movie?
5. Are you in love?
6. Does the camera bother you?
7. Why do you wish to be an actor?
8. What do you like the most about me?

The idea is to mix unemotional, easy questions with some that have more emotional content. Play back the tape without sound, and see if you can pick out the questions by the reaction of the actor. (See Exercise 2 before showing playback.) Then, play the tape with sound, closing your eyes. Be aware of the time between the questions and the answer, study the thinking process. The same goes for an emotional question. After this, play the tape in a normal manner, looking at the whole performance.

A more advanced version has the off-camera questioner ask follow-up questions on the same subject. For example:

Q. Where is Mount Everest?
A. I don't know.
Q. Is it in Canada?
A. I don't think so.
Q. Could you take a guess as to where it is?

A. I really don't know.

Q. Think!

The questioner becomes an interrogator, thus adding another element to the game.

One would hope that reacting was the direct result of listening. Unfortunately, this isn't true. Even in exercises such as the one above, the clever actor will play the game intellectually and remain uninvolved emotionally. The fact is that listening is safe; reacting is not. You can listen technically, but reacting demands involvement. *Note:* See Exercise 2 before viewing playback.

When actors see themselves for the first time on playback, they have many reactions. Most are self conscious, giving nervous giggles, and embarrassed denials. Some can't take it and close their eyes. These reactions, even though they are modified by the presence of the group, are honest.

EXERCISE 2: VIDEOTAPE REACTIONS

Videotape the actors watching themselves on video in the previous listening exercise. Then, play back that tape.

Note that the actors watch their images with a critical eye that has nothing to do with artistic judgment. They see their physical faults, their hopes and ambitions; they see how others might see them, and most important, they see a history of themselves right up to the very moment they have just experienced.

Their reactions are not to mere words, but to a myriad of complex ideas and emotions. An actor, in character, must be able to listen and react in a similar fashion. Because of the camera and its ability to discover the lie, an actor has to learn to overcome the fear of being known and vulnerable.

If the character inhabits you, but part of you has been withdrawn, you are cheating the character.

> *When an actor has a phone conversation in one of my pictures, I always put the other actor off-camera doing their part of the conversation. It isn't that I don't trust the on-camera actor to be able to act out the conversation with the appropriate pauses, etc. It's just that somehow it isn't real unless they are actually having a phone conversation.*
>
> *Norman Jewison*

EXERCISE 3: THE PHONE CALL

Actors ONE and TWO sit side by side, and both look into camera. They must memorize their lines word for word. Before performing the exercise, each actor decides on what subtext he will use in the scene. But each actor keeps this information secret until they have done the scene and the playback session is over.

> ONE
>
> Hi.

> TWO
>
> Hi.

> ONE
>
> I'm calling to say good-bye.

> TWO
>
> Oh?

> ONE
>
> It's just uh . . . well uh . . .

> TWO
>
> I'm in the middle of something.

> ONE
>
> Oh . . . I'm sorry.

> TWO
>
> It's OK. . . . Go on . . . you were saying?

> ONE
>
> If you're busy I'll call back.

> TWO
>
> Look. I just said it's OK.

> ONE
>
> It isn't OK. It never is OK. I'm calling to say something important, and you're telling me you're in the middle of something.

> TWO
>
> Just hold it. Let's just calm down.

```
                    ONE
      I'm calm . . . I'm very calm.


                    TWO
      Good.


There is a long pause after ONE hangs the phone up.

                    TWO
      So . . . you're going on a trip?
      . . . Hello?


TWO hangs up
```

END OF SCENE

Before playback, each actor reveals his subtext. After playback and discussion of whether or not they succeeded, they play the scene again, this time with an objective they have both agreed on in advance. That is, they share the knowledge of who they are and what their relationship is. The actors then should examine the difference between the first version and the one where the objective was shared.

The latter should have moments of emotional history where the unspoken words take on more significance. The reactions then emanate from a personal knowledge of the other's character. The subtext, not the words, should become the important element.

Write similar scenes using this technique, and again see if you can tell the difference between shared objectives and separate ones.

There is a caution to doing scenes written especially for exercise purposes. The actor tends to become lazy or a so-called soap-opera actor. I think the reason for this is the scene's lack of pedigree. There is no play, no plot, no famous author to authenticate the words; one has only the words themselves. So the actor, trying to give the role importance and meaning, may overemphasize the drama and make it into melodrama. The only thing to do is to be aware of the danger and try to take steps to overcome it. This is not to denigrate actors on soaps in any way, as there are a lot of very fine actors in that area, but rather to point out a kind of naturalism that has become a soap-opera style of acting.

When you watch a soap opera, you'll notice that scenes very often end with a closeup of a character immediately after a confrontation with another character. The camera stays on the shot for a long time. The actor is required to react specifically to what has just happened. The last line heard is usually provocative enough to help the actor. But after a second or two, she resorts to pretending to think. Like pretending to listen, pretending to think may work on stage, but never on camera. This condition can easily be recognized when the actor consciously makes facial moves: lips pursing, eyes moving, tongue in cheek, and so on. Her acting becomes technical. Her motivation is no longer the text but rather the time needed for the music to swell and the picture to fade. The next time you watch a soap, look for this shot. Compare it with the reaction shots in the movies named at the end of the chapter.

EXERCISE 4: PHONE CALL # 2

> The actor on camera is in CLOSEUP and listens. The speaking actor off camera is: (1) mother, (2) lover, (3) someone the listener doesn't really like. The off camera actor speaks the lines exactly the same way each time. Do the 3 versions one after the other without stopping.

> > SPEAKING ACTOR
> > Well, I'm glad you finally answered. We were all kind of worried. I've been thinking about what you said. Maybe you're right. Maybe things did get a little out of hand. But I don't think that I'm entirely to blame. I know I said some things. . . . I was just angry. Anyway, you left so abruptly, I didn't have a chance to say anything. We'll get together and talk about it. . . . You'll see. Everything will be OK.

END OF SCENE

Look for the subtle differences, depending on who speaks. Perhaps for the mother and lover the listening actor may find a place to change direction, that is, making a new choice. The main thing is not to play just one emotion. You may also substitute another type of character for the speaker.

The criterion, once again, is honesty. Do you believe it? Is the actor truly listening and then reacting? Most important: Does the camera, in closeup, reveal character every single moment?

EXERCISE 5: THE NEWSPAPER

While someone reads the newspaper off camera, the on-camera listener at some point stops listening. This must be done with no discernible or obvious behavior. No eyes wandering, no long sighs. No movement whatsoever. On playback, the viewers must detect when the moment occurs, but save the discussion until the scene is finished.

Videos to watch with particular regard for listening and reacting:

City Lights: Directed by Charles Chaplin. This is a silent picture with a broad style, but there are scenes at the end—the last five minutes in particular—in which Chaplin, who also starred, truly shows what the thinking actor can do without words.

Reversal of Fortune: Directed by Barbet Schroeder. Jeremy Irons, as the passive observer in his own drama, gives a taciturn character a variety of emotion.

Sophie's Choice: Directed by Alan J. Pakula. Meryl Streep, one of the great technicians of all time, is also a wonderful actress. Note the variety of choices she makes throughout the film, especially when she listens.

Inherit the Wind: Directed by Stanley Kramer. Spencer Tracy is a master at listening. The student actor could watch any of his films to learn the craft.

3 □□□ □□□ □□□

Blocking and Business

Definition

I'll begin by defining what I mean by blocking and business. Blocking is determining where you physically move during a scene. It is the choreography of acting. Business is what you do in the confines of the blocking.

In one scene, for example, the actor walks to the desk, picks up the phone book, and riffles through it. After a pause, he puts down the phone book and takes up a picture frame.

The blocking is the walk to the desk. Business is the picking up and putting down of the phone book and the picking up of the picture frame. Simply put, blocking is where you go, and business is what you do when you get there. When you apply this to the real world of acting, it translates to this: The director can tell you where to go, but it's usually up to you to do something when you get there.

Technical Blocking

Stage performance gives an actor a lot more freedom than film performance does. While it is true that in plays the actor does certain bits of business on specific lines, there is room for variation each time he performs. The stage actor can walk to within 3 feet of a door or, if he chooses, he can make it 2 feet. The 1-foot difference will not be noticed or, for that matter, ever be noticed.

As a film actor, however, you cannot take that kind of license. That 1-foot discrepancy almost always will make the director yell, "Cut!" The reason is purely technical. It has nothing to do with how well or badly you acted. The fact is that cameras do not see like human beings. The camera lens can keep only a certain amount of detail in focus. During rehearsal, the camera assistant measures the distances from the lens to you, the actor. He marks down these distances, and to accommodate them, he moves the lens to adjust the focus. So, if you move to 3 feet from the door in rehearsal, and then, on the take, move just to 2 feet, the chances are you will be out of focus because of the limitations of the lens.

When shooting a film, the actors mark a scene for the camera crew just so they can get these measurements. Marking a scene means that the actor goes through the motions, just saying the lines without emotion, so the technical problems can be solved. On big-budget pictures, the stars usually have their stand-ins do most of this work. (A stand-in is a person who marks the scene for the actor.) But when it comes closer to the time to do the scene, the star also participates in a technical rehearsal, and for good reason. Besides the camera operator, the sound and boom person need a rehearsal so they can get a volume check and make sure their microphones can pick up the dialogue and stay out of camera range.

As a good actor, you can use this time to do your own homework. You can measure the number of steps it takes to get to the door. You can make a note always to turn the same way on each rehearsal. Most important, you can assure the technical people that you will give them no surprises when it comes time to shoot.

Technical mistakes can rob the actor of precious energy. To go through a take, getting the emotions right where you want them, only to hear a "Cut!" because you wandered out of camera range, is not only frustrating, but very expensive. It is no accident they call it the movie business. Time is money, and on a movie set, it's big money.

Scenes in film and television are usually shot first as masters. In a master shot, the camera can see most of action in the scene, and the actors get to do the scene from beginning to end, establishing the moves and actions they must repeat when the coverage is shot.

Coverage is the sum total of all the other shots of the same scene that isolate certain elements. The master scene, for example, takes place between two people sitting on a sofa. One gets up and goes to the door, pauses there for a line, and then leaves. The coverage could include the following shots:

1. A medium shot of Actor One on the sofa from Actor Two's point of view.
2. A similar medium shot of Actor Two from Actor One's point of view.
3. A closeup of Actor One.
4. A closeup of Actor Two.
5. A pan or moving shot as Actor One goes to the door and turns.
6. A reversal of the previous shot to show Actor Two still sitting on the couch.
7. A shot of Actor One leaving.

Now this could be a 2-minute scene, but without any retakes, the actors perform the same scene, or portions of it, seven times. Now some of you will say,

"Part of the time the camera isn't even on me!" True, but it doesn't mean you can let down on your performance. Imagine yourself as the on-camera actor with your partner not giving any emotion to the scene. You would have a hard time giving a convincing performance. The fact is, you're always on, whether or not the camera is pointing at you. Dirk Bogarde was said to get into costume and makeup just to help his fellow actors do reaction shots.

The technical details of blocking must become automatic so you can attack the performance with a clear mind. The movements also must be done with a sense of spontaneity. Many times I have heard actors complain that this regimented behavior is the death of creativity. Their philosophy would have you believe that all creation is haphazard, wanton, and capricious. They may claim that Stravinsky didn't bother to learn counterpoint, Picasso couldn't draw the figure, and actors are born, not made. The facts are just the opposite. What good is a film or television performance if the actor is constantly out of focus and can't be heard?

The technical aspects of acting for film such as hitting marks are not the goal, but rather one means of reaching the goal. You might wish to be a great hockey player, but you should learn how to skate first.

Artistic Blocking Technique

All actions have a reason. Everything you do is logical or creates its own logic. The blocking is intrinsic to the meaning of the scene. You do not answer the phone unless you hear it ring. And if, in collaboration with the director, you cannot make each action justified and reasonable, you must question the move or action.

An old theatrical joke goes like this:

Actor: What's my motivation?
Director: You'll do it because I told you to.

So . . . you get a piece of business, and you can't find a reason to justify it. The director listens to your arguments and then says, "Just do it!"

You can quit. You can do it automatically. Or you can invent a reason and use it to get by. It may be a stretch or feel strange to you, but it will work. This is a rare event, but I can assure you it will happen sometime. Norman Jewison said that when he encounters an actor who has trouble with the blocking or with handling a prop, he tries to change things to make the actor comfortable. But, he adds, sometimes no change is possible. You must prepare for those moments.

Good directors know what the camera sees, and they block for that. They also block for editing. So, there may be a spot in the scene that seems uncomfortable. When you mention it, the director tells you to forget it because it won't be used. It is just a device to get you from one place to the other to facilitate the editing. You must accept that vision. It is very difficult for actors in a scene to imagine what the edited version will be like.

Stella Adler, in her book *The Technique of Acting*, states, "The prop is always truthful." I believe that the use of the prop should always be truthful. Unfortunately this is often not the case.

Actors grab props and fiddle with them because they feel nervous, and their hands are not communicating with their brains. The rest of the body may be in character, but for some reason, hands, and to a lesser extent, arms, live a life totally removed from the character. A lot of actors use a very simple cure—they put their hands in their pockets. The next time you go to a community playhouse, notice how often the men, particularly, shove their hands in their pockets. This problem is solvable, but it takes real concentration.

Situation

Two characters who are best friends, one telling the other—played by you—about something important. During the scene you invent a bit of business. You pick up a box of matches and look at the printing on it. The other actor talks on, and you put the matches down.

The audience could analyze the business in many ways, but here are just two possibilities.

One: You have told the audience that you are distracted by the matches, which could mean that what the other character is saying is not important to you.

Two: The matches make a significant point in the plot, and you have just discovered this meaning by accident. You break in excitedly and tell what you have discovered.

In both instances the audience is going to watch you pick up the matches and wonder why you did it. Your action will compel the audience to watch. If you put the matches down and the scene goes on with no more reference to them, you have created a rude and bored character. Remember that you were supposed to be friends at the beginning of the scene. You saw the matches and without much thought picked them up. The consequences of this action didn't occur to you. You just followed the old adage, "idle hands are the devil's workshop."

Your simple action could take the audience away from the scene and thus ruin it. Your friend's words are meant to be important.

Let's take a brief moment to explain the various shots. A master shot used to mean a full length view of the actors. But modern directors sometimes use closeups and medium shots as masters. I would define a modern master shot as one where most of the action can be seen by the camera and the scene can play from beginning to end without a break.

A closeup is usually defined as a head and shoulder view. An extreme closeup is just the face, or the eyes. Medium shots are from the waist up. A two shot is of two people and logically, a medium two shot is two people from the waist up. None of these shots are exact as each director may define what they encompass.

A good general rule for shooting the exercises in this book is to be as close as possible to better observe the actor's reactions.

You must realize that in a medium two shot, your hands appear 2 feet high on the screen. You must also take into account that when your eyes—your focus—go away from the other actor, you are telling the audience something whether you want to or not. You are drawing attention to yourself. *You are stealing the scene.*

If you accept the fact that the words are important, it becomes necessary for you to behave accordingly. You can't expect the audience to believe things that you contradict by your actions.

That's what the actor does who, as another character is speaking to him, looks for lint on his jacket or fiddles with his glasses. Some of the older stars were famous for variations on these bits. Scene-stealing distractions were the very reason W.C. Fields hated to act in scenes with dogs or children.

During your preparation, you should make notes of what you want to do and where you want to do it. You should be prepared to defend your deeds with irrefutable dramatic logic. You must also differentiate between blocking moves and pieces of business. Blocking moves, for the most part, fill the requirements of the director. Blocking is the choreography that allows creative choices in the editing process. Pieces of business, on the other hand, are the small extras that can make an extraordinarily effective characterization.

Individuals behave in unique ways. Their feelings can manifest themselves overtly, thus adding a dimension to the character. Such behavior can be barely visible, yet influence the total performance. In *Midnight Cowboy*, Dustin Hoffman decided to play the part of Ratso Rizzo with a very painful-looking limp. His limp looked like the result of a childhood injury. Ratso was a down-and-out hustler who would sell his own mother for a quarter. Yet at the end of the movie I found myself in tears over his death. I believe that most audiences reacted the same way. The sight of this pathetic limp created a reservoir of good will. In spite of Ratso's despicable character, the audience forgave him his sins, and I believe they did it for one reason. The painful limp contributed to what he was, and because of that, they could understand. I don't believe any modern hero that wretched or rotten has ever evoked such sympathy. I don't think Mr. Hoffman would have achieved the same effect had he strutted through the movie on two normal legs. It was reported that he put sharp pebbles in one shoe to remind himself to limp. However he did it, the business paid off. The character Ratso had a limp that affected his life and in turn affected the audience.

Actors who make strong choices regarding overt behavioral characteristics had better have equally strong reasons for making them. You can almost make it a rule: If you're going to do something big, you had better have an equally big reason for doing it!

Jack Lemmon tells a story about making the film, *The Apartment*. His character has a cold in a scene with actor Fred MacMurray.

> *Well, I decided to use a nasal spray. Now I'm all nervous because I think he's not going to give me a raise because he knows I've been letting executives use my apartment for hanky panky . . . . Well . . . the prop man puts milk in the nasal spray because the picture's in black and white, and when the spray shoots out, you'll really see it. I didn't say anything to Fred or to Billy Wilder, the director, and we start the scene. In the script, Fred lets me off the hook, and I'm so excited I squeeze the spray right under his nose. And all Fred did was look at it and do a slow take, following the spray until it hit the floor and then back to me. You hardly notice it on the screen, but for those who did, it was perfect. It was subtle. If it was a big thing, then it would be a gag. But it happened in the context of the scene and the characters. It was legitimate."*
>
> *Jack Lemmon*

Legitimate . . . credible . . . real . . . honest . . . these words will occur again and again. They are as important to blocking and business as to any other aspect of acting. That's why it's extremely important to rehearse with the items you are actually going to use—even though that nasal spray was a surprise that succeeded. Scrutinize the set or the location. Make a mental inventory of what is there. Chances are you'll have nothing to do with 99 percent of the stuff, but it's all usable.

EXERCISE 6: BLOCKING

In rehearsing the following scene, the actors should each hit four marks taped on the floor at least four feet apart. During the performance, someone monitors the actors' success or failure in hitting the marks by simply watching their feet and making notes. Since a video camera has such a wide range of focus, it will be impossible to tell by the picture playback whether the actors are in or out of focus. But I can assure you that with a movie camera any missing of the marks would ruin a take.

One enters, very upset. Two watches as One searches for something.

> ONE
> O.K. Where is it?

> TWO
> Where is what?

> ONE
> That's what I truly like about
> you. You always answer a ques-
> tion with a question.

> TWO
> And you always say always.

> ONE
> What I always say is a direct
> result of what you always say.

> TWO
> So what you're saying is we have
> a symbiotic relationship.

One stops searching and comes to two.

> ONE
> Are you putting me on?

> TWO
> Am I putting you on what?

> ONE
> There! You did it again!

One walks away and searches.

> TWO
> If you'd keep better tabs on
> things you wouldn't lose them.

> ONE
> That's like saying if I knew
> where things were, they wouldn't
> be lost.

> TWO
> Exactly.

One stops and looks at Two.

                  ONE
      You know where they are don't
      you?

                  TWO
      Yes.

                  ONE
      And you let me look like a fool.

                  TWO
      It breaks up the day.

                  ONE
      O.K., where are they?

Two holds up the keys. One takes them and leaves.

                              END OF SCENE

The actors should repeat this scene until they can hit all of the marks without being obvious. They must actually land on each mark, not merely come close. The body and face must be within inches of the same position each time they do the scene.

The next scene is an exercise for business. Handling props naturally is a must. The film actor must be able to do repeated takes making sure that the props hit their marks each time. The routine is set at rehearsal and should never change after the first take unless the director requests something different. In this scene, each actor decides when the business occurs and performs so it can happen in a credible manner. The dialogue indicates the business.

EXERCISE 7: BUSINESS

Needed props: Two glasses. Optional props: magazines, ash tray. Shoot scene as a master.

                  ONE
      We really don't know if it was
      murder or suicide.

                    TWO
I know.

                    ONE
Yeah?

                    TWO
Yeah.

                    ONE
How do you know?

                    TWO
I just know.

                    ONE
I don't believe you.

                    TWO
I was there.

                    ONE
What?

                    TWO
I was there when it happened.

                    ONE
But you told the police . . .

                    TWO
I know what I told the police.

                    ONE
Why? . . . Why did you lie?

                    TWO
I have my reasons.

                    ONE
Why did you tell me?

                    TWO
Can't you guess?

              ONE
It . . . it wasn't suicide.

              TWO
No.

              ONE
It was murder.

              TWO
Good guess.

              ONE
And you did it.

              TWO
Clever person.

              ONE
And you're going to kill me.

              TWO
You're as good as dead.

              ONE
I switched the glasses.

              TWO
I switched them back.

              ONE
I saw you switch them back and
switched them again.

              TWO
That wasn't fair. Oh well.

Two drops dead.

              ONE
Now I know this was suicide
because I was there.

END OF SCENE

The actors must invent ways to make the switches effectively without the other character seeing them. This necessitates the invention of moves and other business to mask the switches, such as picking up a magazine for a look or getting an ash tray. The important thing is to create a believable scene. You should also make note of which hand did what. Learn to handle objects the same way, each take. This way, when it comes time to edit different takes together, objects don't mysteriously jump from one hand to the other.

Blocking and business are techniques of acting, not mere appendages that haphazardly appear at the last minute. Glenn Jordan tells of an actor who had to pour a cup of tea while delivering some very dramatic lines. After several takes, the actor said he couldn't do the business and the lines at the same time. That was ridiculous—what he needed was training.

The actor must control the instrument, in this case the body. Take dancing lessons, learn to fence. Practice different kinds of walks and postures. Exercise. The film character's body language is the audience's first clue to who she is. Blocking and business, at the onset, may be just where the person goes and what she does. But in the end, how she does those things should be organic to the character.

Films to Study

Midnight Cowboy: Directed by John Schlesinger. Both Dustin Hoffman and Jon Voight move effectively.

On the Waterfront: Directed by Elia Kazan. Marlon Brando as an ex-prize fighter creates the character just by walking down the street.

Reversal of Fortune: Directed by Barbet Schroeder. Watch Glenn Close's walk and body language.

4

Preparation

Stage to Film

To "get into the part," the person who trains for stage acting uses any number of techniques—character bios, scene analysis, sense-memory exercises, and research on the play's subject matter for background material. Each one of these techniques is equally appropriate for film and television preparation. But at some point in the process, the film actor should be aware of how the performance is to be done, and this should trigger some unique ideas that apply only to camera techniques.

In the modern theatre you get a lot of deals between the audience and the actor: I'll pretend this is really happening if you pretend to believe it. And it's not a very clean deal. People are not very comfortable with that. But they've gotten used to it.

Mike Nichols

A theatre audience accepts a new, tenuous reality as soon as they become involved with the play. The better the performance, the writing, and set design, the deeper the acceptance.

I think the "deals" Mr. Nichols is talking about have more to do with the limitations of the theatre genre itself. Whereas a stage play may often refer to big events that occur offstage, the film must show them. Whereas the stage actor is allowed a poetic voice whose words paint the picture, the film actor is actually *in* the picture, and the telling is almost superfluous. The stage setting may consist of fragments and symbols; it is the rare film that doesn't emulate reality.

One often hears, "I'm an actor, I can play anything." More often than not, when it applies to theatre, this is quite true. If the actor creates an illusion skillfully, the audience will accept it. In the theatre, men play women, women play men, men and women play animals, and so forth.

This theatrical license is an essential part of many play productions. But even the most naturalistic play still has theatrical elements. By *theatrical* in no sense do I mean overblown, amateurish acting, exaggerated gestures, and florid speech.

Let me define what I do mean by the word theatrical. After a play is written, rehearsed, rewritten, and fine-tuned, the next logical step is the performance. This begins with the actors preparing in their dressing rooms, the audience taking their seats, and is completed when the actors take their bows and the audience leaves.

This is a theatrical event. I contend that the actor's knowledge of this event has a subconscious effect on preparation, influencing all the techniques he uses in rehearsal. Knowing the size of the theatre and the stage, for instance, has a direct influence on his voice projection and stage blocking.

An actor in a play, when he gets up in the morning, knows that at eight o'clock that night, he will perform. His whole day is geared to that fact. The actor in film has no idea when he will be called upon to do a scene. After the call, it could be 10 minutes or it could be 5 hours. Then, an assistant comes, and there you are in front of the camera, and you have to do it!"

Glenn Jordan

But the actor preparing for film or television should also have a vision of what the "event" will be, the event in this case being the time the performance is shot on film or tape.

In film, unlike the theatre, you're looking for the physical look, the age, the type, even the color of the eyes or the hair. Now you can play parts on stage way past your age. But in film, to accomplish that, we have to go through a tremendous makeup process, prosthetics, and so on all of which is time-consuming and expensive. In other words, casting in a film becomes more intense, more pragmatic.

Norman Jewison

What has this to do with preparation? Everything. *It is essential that actors know who they are and what they look like. They must define themselves before preparation.*

You Are You

It sounds a little superficial, doesn't it, like one of those self-help books. After all, they're not buying you, they're buying your talent. But maybe the real you is nothing like the perceived you. Maybe you think and act tall; you look in the mirror and see a sensitive face and a sweet disposition, yet you're looked upon by some as short, brutish, and sullen.

Will your best friends tell you the awful truth?

The idea of what a leading man or leading woman should look like changes from year to year. So I'm not talking about handsome, good-looking, pretty, beautiful, or any other fashionable quality. But, to be realistic, most actors who become movie stars do have generally appealing physical looks, looks approved by audience tastes.

Knowing who you are and what you look like saves a lot of effort wasted in trying to cram yourself into parts that simply won't work. Prepare for what you believe will be the most likely casting for you; don't practice the violin if you're to give a piano recital. In *No Acting Please* Eric Morris and Joan Hotchkis write: "I came to the realization that while there's lip service paid to using your personal life on stage and getting 'deep' into your own emotions, few actors have the courage to do this and most teachers aren't even aware of the necessity for this kind of search."

The following exercise is not meant to reveal your innermost secrets, nor does it necessitate an intrusion into your privacy. The personal questions have to do with your public self: your self-perception. It is your choice as to how far you wish to go in answering.

EXERCISE 8: WHO AM I?

Prepare a list. Then, on camera, recite.

1. Give your body measurements—feet, legs, torso, arms, hips, waist, head, height.
2. Describe your eyes, teeth, hair, complexion, and smile.
3. Describe your interests, likes and dislikes, hobbies, and goals.
4. Describe what's best and what's worst about yourself, and what you would most like to change.
5. Describe where you wish to be 10 years from now.
6. Describe what you are doing to attain your goals.

After playback, first ask yourself whether or not you stand by the answers. Then, frankly and gently, the group tells where they agree and disagree. This will undoubtedly lead to a few bad jokes, but since all members of the group must participate, whoever gives will be in line to take.

The necessity of complete honesty in this exercise correlates with one specific fact in the film and television world: because of the way film and television are cast, you will, more often than not, be playing characters that resemble you, both physically and emotionally. When the audience first sees you on the screen, their first impression should define your character.

Olivier said the character inhabits you, and I believe it is your person that is cast in film and television. It is you and the vision of you in the part that stimulate the director to want to see more. Typecasting may be the pejorative word to describe it, but you'll come to accept it as a part of the business. Like it or not, you'll be thought as a type and there'll be auditions where you'll be dismissed without having a chance to read. This is a lot more satisfactory than the perfunctory audition. That's one where the director talks on the phone while you're auditioning.

Most actors begin their careers by doing bit parts—a couple of lines, screentime, 2 minutes or even less. The actor is usually handed only the pages of script that encompass her part. Through begging, getting lucky, or knowing someone, you may be able to get your hands on the whole script. But don't count on it. The problem is to know how you fit into the mosaic. Don't ever think that a measly two lines can't get you noticed. It has before, and it will again. Careers have been launched with less.

You'll undoubtedly read for the part and generally know who the character is. So, when you're cast, the first thing to do is to research whatever job or situation your character is involved in.

> Pudovkin, the Russian director, believed if you wanted an actor to play a policeman, why don't you hire a policeman? Because he will behave and do exactly what he does every day, and he will be more believable than an actor trying to play a policeman. That works fine until it comes time for the real policeman to say lines. . . . So, in a film, the director is often looking for someone that maybe doesn't have the experience of a well-known actor, but he will overlook that if he can get someone who is perfect for the part in his mind's eye.
>
> Norman Jewison

Let's say you're cast as a detective. All of us have seen detectives in film and TV time and time again. And each of us has a clichéd idea about how they should behave. To avoid these clichés, you should first examine what detectives really do.

> You have to know how to talk to actors. Directors who don't, talk to them about feeling, but directors who do, will talk to them about doing. You don't ever say to an actor, "Get mad at this guy." What you might say is, "You let that person know, if he tries this again, you're going to murder him. And make damn sure that you see in his eyes, and he understands how serious you are." Because that's a do-able thing. You can take a nonactor, and if you can get him to relax emotionally and think a thought, you'll see it with the camera. You couldn't do that onstage.
>
> Sydney Pollack

The key phrase is "a do-able thing." You must know what your character—in this case, a detective—does. You must also know that besides being a detective, the person is a human being as well. Too often, an actor picks up the aura of a profession, and gives a one-dimensional performance.

As soon as you read *detective*, you probably thought of film and television detectives, not the real thing. Most of us have seen a lot of movies, and we are prejudiced by them. We've seen every profession portrayed, cowboys, senators, rich people, poor people. You may not consciously remember the actor in the part, but chances are, the impression of the role has made its mark. In the detective category, the private eye has become a cliché. But let's say you're not playing Sam Spade or Phillip Marlowe—what do you do?

Your concept should begin with what a detective does, then proceed to what unique characteristics you can add to the part.

One caution: be wary of simulating nothing but the truth. Most of the detective's work is plain dull. It entails endless paperwork, boring interviews, and long hours when nothing happens. You can be sure the script will not reflect that side of the detective's life. Yet, as a good actor, you are trying to be real and honest. Even with chases, car crashes, and dead bodies every 5 minutes, it is possible.

The trick is to let the script speak for itself. Put your character into that world. Don't try to enhance it. Just live in it. With your solid preparation, your character exists truthfully, no matter how unreal some of the situations may be. A good example of this truthfulness was a TV show called "Cop Rock," which was a noble failure. "Cop Rock" had some fine acting and a lot of unusual acting situations. For instance, many times the drama stopped while the actors went into a wild rock-and-roll musical number, complete with choreography. Then, after the song finished, they went right back into the drama. The scenes were as real as you can get. The musical numbers were devised as script continuations, but, nevertheless, they were interruptions. The actors never lost focus, but reacted truthfully to situations, no matter how unusual.

Much more often, though, the actor is cast in a weekly program that has conventional dramatic parameters, which, to be generous, are not exactly Shakespearian. Still, you can't change the destiny of the program by offering literary suggestions to make it better. Just by acting your part better, you'll accomplish all that you can.

As the saying goes, "There are no small parts, there are only small actors." If you make the most of what you have, without going overboard, you're doing your job.

Preparation for featured or starring roles is somewhat more complex. Now you have the whole script, and you know the story. What do you do?

I read the script over and over again. First I try to understand what the script means, and once I think I understand what it means, overall, then I read it once more, concentrating on my character's lines. I read it aloud, not trying to give the lines any expression; just to familiarize myself with the words. I want the words to be familiar in my head so when I finally do them in performance, they come easily and naturally. Then I come to the first day of rehearsal. I put my script in front of me, no matter how familiar I am with it. When another character speaks to me, first, I will listen, then I will let whatever reaction that creates happen. I won't force this reaction. After this, I'll check my reply in the script, look at the other actor, and say my line. From the beginning, I will start contact with the other actor and let my performance come out of a combination of the emotions they stir in me, the text itself, and the guidance the director offers.

Don Murray

Out of Order

One of the most difficult acting problems in film and television is caused by the simple fact that scripts are shot out of order. Page 30 on Monday . . . Page 12 on Tuesday. On Page 30, you're locked in a mental ward for the criminally insane. On Page 12, you're a happily married churchgoer. That means you're at the dramatic peak of the whole story the day before you shoot the "build."

I've exaggerated these plot circumstances a bit—most scripts don't have such a drastic change. But that makes your job even more difficult. The more subtle the change, the harder it is to solve the acting problem. It is essential to plot an emotional strategy throughout a script. Because so many times you're doing scenes back and forth in time, you must know where your character is at any given moment.

The director approaches a scene with the whole film in mind. It is our job to see how this scene fits into the mosaic. The director is the only person who knows what effect the whole film will have on an audience. At least, theoretically we hope that's so. The actor is saying, "Wait a minute, I wouldn't do that. Why would I do that?" That's when I have to say, "You do that because don't you remember on Page 4, that such and such happened. And we haven't shot that yet. Let's go back and read the pages that affect this scene." You should constantly go back and do your homework while they're setting up, so you know where you're going to be emotionally. . . . Sometimes actors don't do that. They play each scene separately. That's why directors and actors have to have a very close relationship—a little bit closer than it is in the theatre.

Norman Jewison

Before continuing, it may be best to explain why film and television movies are not usually shot in the order they're written—*TIME AND MONEY*. If the crew is on the set, ready to shoot, it is more efficient to shoot all subsequent scenes that take place on that same set. All of the scenes that take place in the living room, let's say, will be shot while the crew is in that locale. This means all the crew members must make notes on all sorts of technical things pertaining to where each scene occurs in the story.

For example, they must note the time of year, the actors' wardrobes and hair styles, and the set design. And like these tangible things, the actors' comprehension of story and character must fit into a logical time line. Audiences must not be aware of the hodgepodge of filming when they watch the film.

How do you become the character?

You know how you grow mushrooms? You put them in a cold, damp place and you feed them shit. That's basically what acting is. You put out the best set of circumstances that would make it possible for this thing (character) to grow, and then you trust. . . . You really have to be accessible.

Debra Winger

Don't take that word *accessible* to mean that you are a hollow shell waiting for the director to fill in the parts. No director wants puppets. Glenn Jordan states that he always wants the actor to come in with a choice, even if it's wrong. Directors welcome your ideas as long as you have not cast them in cement.

There are some actors who bring in their performance as some sort of a gift that's already wrapped. They prepare in a way that has nothing to do with the director or the other actors. It can be done very skillfully. And sometimes in the film, because of time constraints, some actors do it that way.

Don Murray

Mr. Murray has a point. You get the part Thursday night for a Friday morning start. You'll meet the other actors in makeup, and if you're lucky, you'll get a chance to run lines. On the set, you have a couple of walk-throughs to set the blocking, and then the director calls for a take. What happens now really depends on what happened in your preparation last night.

Using the script as a blueprint, the actor first notes all major plot changes—the points at which something happens that sends the story off in another direction. Then, within those major changes, the actor creates a subtext, noting, the reasons, emotional and textual behind the character's behavior. The actor should also look for possibilities of making subtle differences in the way she reacts to a different characters. Is this the kind of person who is brusque to waitresses and obsequious to policemen?

These notes need not be extensive. In fact, one-word clues can be suffi-
cient. The problem with going on and on, writing essays on character, is this:
the brain takes over. An intellectual analysis is fine as long as you remember
that characters, even very smart characters, behave the way they do because
of feelings. Some may repress them magnificently, but they're still there.

One other thing to note: Ask yourself why the other characters behave the
way they do toward you. Mike Nichols stated in an interview: "When I teach
acting, I tell my students that it's important not to make up your mind about
your character, not to present the audience with a conclusion, because something closed is not as interesting or alive as something open. And people are
endlessly surprising. Surely the greatest thing in a character, whether in a book
or a play or a movie, is just that: the sense of surprise."

I'm quite sure that Nichols wants the actor to prepare, but to leave space
for things to happen. As Don Murray said, "Don't bring the gift in all neatly
packaged." Lazy actors bring neither the gift nor the preparation. Their rationale is that talent will see them through. They assure the director that it will
"be there" when the camera rolls. Too many times this lack of preparation is
accepted because the director casts an actor from seeing a past performance
and feels a wary trust. My feeling is that there are a lot of talented actors in
this world, and most directors prefer the ones who come prepared.

Re: When lines should be known in rehearsal.

*The freedom of improvisation was last week, and you can't get that freedom
back unless you have mastery of the material. The spur of the moment has to
come of actually knowing what is and what isn't.*

Peter Brook

One last word about preparation: Know the locale, the time of the year,
and why you are there. Do this, no matter how small the part. Finally, know
your lines, and what the character's objective is in each scene, and, of course,
listen and react.

Like a jazz musician, you should know the tune, the chords, and the
structure—then you may improvise. This does not mean paraphrasing the script.
Paraphrasing is a bad habit born of poor technique and inflated ego. The actor
who doesn't bother to learn the lines as written usually makes the excuse that
they were poorly written. Once the habit is begun, it is very difficult to stop.
Then a situation may arise where the director wrote the script or the writer
is present and there you are, compelled to say the lines as written for the first
time. If you have trouble with a line, try to find a way to make it work. But
if you can't solve the problem, discuss it with the director. Don't improvise
unless the director suggests it.

A lot of actors take short cuts in preparation and succeed. To my mind, this is a risky approach and can backfire seriously. You could give one brilliant performance, but wait years for another.

EXERCISE 9: STAGE VS. FILM PERFORMANCE

One set of actors should prepare the following scene, including blocking as a stage performance. Another group should prepare the scene as a film/television performance. Video the stage performance with a long shot, using a stationary camera. Shoot the film performance much closer; move the camera if you wish.

> ONE
> If I said that I was very, very
> ill, what would you think?

> TWO
> I'd think you had AIDS.

> ONE
> Right. . . . And what else would
> you think?

> TWO
> I'd think you were gay.

> ONE
> Then what else?

> TWO
> And you hadn't said anything to
> me.

> ONE
> Betrayed, huh?

> TWO
> Nothing that drastic.

> ONE
> You're prejudiced.

> TWO
> I am not.

> **ONE**
> You have a clichéd, prejudicial mind.

> **TWO**
> Why? Because I associated AIDS with gays?

> **ONE**
> Exactly. What if you're wrong about me?

> **TWO**
> What if! What if you get the hell out of here. Go play your games with someone else.

> **ONE**
> No one else has such an interest. Is that clear or do I have to spell it out?

> **TWO**
> You've given it to me.

> **ONE**
> That's funny.

> **TWO**
> You bastard! My God . . . Oh my God! How could you do that?

> **ONE**
> I know you'll deny it, but I want you to know that I know what you did. I just wanted to see whether or not you'd try to put the blame on me.

> **TWO**
> You're OK?

> **ONE**
> No thanks to you. I've waited a long time for you to say something.

One starts out.

>   ONE
>   I hope it was worth it.

>   TWO
>   Matter of fact it was.

>   ONE
>   I guess we'll just have to wait
>   to find out. See you.

>   TWO
>   We used protection.

>   ONE
>   Did you?

>   TWO
>   . . . No. . . . look at the
>   odds.

>   ONE
>   I don't have to. You're the one
>   who's taken the gamble.

One leaves. Two reacts.

END OF SCENE

I've chosen a hot dramatic subject so the actors can better differentiate between the two versions.

You should try to ignore the filming techniques and concentrate on the acting. Note the difference from line to line. Even if the characters in each version have no correlation, look for the technique in each. Do the gestures, the relationships, the connections vary because of the film-versus-stage performance? Would the stage version as it was performed still seem as if it were for the theatre if you used special camera techniques, such as closeups?

Find out by filming the stage-acting performance again, this time using closeups, and analyze the difference between that and the performed-for-film version. Are the characters in each version equally credible? Are the body language and business in each, natural and meaningful?

Good technique frees the artist to create. A lot of people have said this, but still some students of acting resist. Today's film and television industry is sophisticated, knowledgeable, and cautious. The well-prepared actor has a much better chance of building a career than the seat-of-the-pants talent.

One last word on preparation. Memorizing the part, running lines, and rehearsing blocking and business are certainly a part of preparation. But you must be careful that these very important ingredients don't take over. A more comprehensive description of preparation would be this. You know what the character wants every single moment and have a rationale for each action. You have control and are able to perform whatever the text demands. Last, you have already experienced similar conditions in workshops, exercises, and self-study, so when you are actually cast in a part, you are familiar with the problems.

Too many actors prepare only after they are cast in a part. The smart actor prepares each day for that eventuality.

5

Character

I believe the main difference in creating character for film versus stage is this: The stage actor paints broad strokes, looking for the whole physical impression; the film actor begins with small details, looking for the hidden traits. The stage actor wears the character's clothes, while the film actor not only wears the clothes, but has sewn the button—the one that doesn't quite match—on the sleeve. It doesn't matter what condition the stage actor's fingernails are in, but show me the well-manicured hand of a foundry worker in a film, and I'll ask a lot of questions.

The Building Blocks

Small details accumulate, and when there are enough of them, they create a reality. In Dirk Bogarde's wonderful book, *Snakes and Ladders*, he states: "I'm an actor who works from the outside in, rather than the reverse. Once I can wear the clothes which my alter-ego has chosen to wear, I then begin the process of his development from inside the layers. . . . [concerning wardrobe on *The Servant*] Each item . . . was carefully chosen by Losey, [the director, Joseph Losey] down to the tie-pin: a tight, shiny, blue serge suit, black shoes which squeaked a little, lending a disturbing sense of secret arrival, porkpie hat with a Jay's feather, a Fair Isle sweater, shrunken, darned at the elbows, a nylon scarf with horses' heads and stirrups. A mean shabby outfit for a mean and shabby man."

In film, it's more likely than on stage that if the script says *antique vase*, it will be just that. So many films today are shot on location that the streets, the buildings, and even the rooms function in real life as they do in the film. It is the actor's job to fit into these environments as if he belonged there.

Quoting again in *Snakes and Ladders* Dirk Bogarde writes that "with Losey, one also discovered the value of textures. The textures of things; of wood, of metal, of glass, of the petals of a flower, the paper of a simple playing card, of snow even, and fabric. Plaster wood, however well combed, does not feel like wood, neither does it photograph like wood; nylon is not silk, fiber glass is not steel, a canvas door does not close with the satisfying sound or weight of mahogany. All these apparently trivial items, or obvious if you like, add up to an enormous whole. And the actor feels the reality. It is, of course, totally cinematic, not theatrical. In the theatre almost nothing must be real. It is reality extended.

The process of building a character is complex. There is no magic formula, no method that guarantees success. But it is this very complexity that intrigues us. Like all human beings, characters have good days and bad. They behave in a consistent way, then all of sudden change direction. They are in constant flux, because stimuli change from moment to moment. Or they resist change and become rigid. Even the most passive and boring character must still be interesting enough for the audience to watch. One supposes the writer had a strong dramatic reason to write about that person, and it is the actor's job to fulfill that mission, and indeed, to enhance it.

It is the rare actor who can read a part and know, from that moment on, what she is going to do. The danger in such an act is this—the insight hits with a bang. You rehearse it and solidify it, then, just as quickly as it came, you suddenly know that it is wrong. The process of undoing is more painful than doing. When you work on a character in one way and then change your mind, you may end up with a hybrid character, which in itself is fine, except that you may have lost control. That is, you may switch from one to another choice during performance without being aware of it.

I prefer a slow, meticulous process, making note of each detail and adding one item to another until you know who the character is. The cumulative building of character helps you to reject or accept ideas as you go along. Debra Winger states in an *American Film* interview, "I think the biggest thing an actor can learn is trust—to trust that something is going to happen." In short, do your homework and be patient.

It would be interesting to get a part on Monday and wake up on Tuesday as the character. It is no longer your bed, your toothbrush, your clothes, but the character's. Your friends and relatives are now the character's. Your itches, the taste in your mouth, and the smells of the morning are no longer yours.

In this Kafkaesque dream, you have ceased to exist. The question is, Does an actor have to give up self to play a part? I don't think so. You must learn to make intelligent decisions about the character and then figure out how to implement them with action.

You have to make choices. No director in the world can help you with that.
They can reject what they don't like, but they're yours. You're using your craft
eventually, but all the craft in the world won't help you make choices.

Gene Hackman

Intellect and Instinct

A lot of actors make character bios, which is fine. But first, it is important to know the character's philosophy and attitude about the following subjects:

1. Sex
2. Religion
3. Morality
4. Social customs
5. Mortality

The traits or observable manners of a character may have nothing to do with this list. Indeed, all of the character's real feelings may be so deeply hidden, so expertly repressed, that we see the exact opposite of what lies beneath. The character may also show different, and contradictory, behavior to other characters. People react to different stimuli, and even though we appear consistent, it only takes a slight diversion to elicit a radical change.

A person who hates the idea of romance, mocks friends in love, and disavows the existence of love may turn the corner and become smitten. Actors must always look for this proverbial corner. A test of true character understanding is for the actor to know what choices the character makes under pressure.

EXERCISE 10: CHARACTER

You're a night clerk in a sleazy hotel. By day you are a university student. The camera is on the clerk. The voice is off camera. Write the clerk's ideas about the five topics just listed before performing the scene. Also, write the clerk's classes, major, and grades.

Begin on Clerk's action (whatever you choose to do).

                    VOICE
          You open?

                    CLERK
          Yes.

                    VOICE
          I want a room.

                    CLERK
          That'll be six bucks.

                    VOICE
          What are you looking at?

                    CLERK
          Nothing.

                    VOICE
          Is there a towel in the room?

                    CLERK
          It's a buck for towels.

                    VOICE
          For six bucks I should get a
          towel.

                    CLERK
          Yeah.

                    VOICE
          Look, I don't have a buck. But I
          want a shower.

                    CLERK
          It's a buck for a towel.

                    VOICE
          Gimme a break.

                    CLERK
          I can't.

                    VOICE
          One lousy towel.

                    CLERK
          I said I can't.

                    VOICE
          Why?

                    CLERK
          They check on me.

                    VOICE
                   (Mocks)
         They check on me.

                    CLERK
         Use your shirt.

                    VOICE
         Thanks.

The clerk watches for a moment.

                    CLERK
         I don't make the damn rules.

                    VOICE
         You just follow them.

                    CLERK
         If I had a dollar I'd get you
         towel.

                    VOICE
         Thanks. See you. . . .

Voice leaves. Clerk goes back to previous action.

                    CLERK
         What do people want from me?

                                    END OF SCENE

The clerk's behavior may or may not reflect some of the ideas about the topics listed. Prepare the scene again. This time the actor should dress the part of the clerk and use props if needed. Before retaping, write down the clerk's answers to the following:

1. Favorite food
2. Self image: clothes, hair; neat, sloppy, fastidious, and so on.
3. Favorite writer
4. Favorite music
5. Major peeves

Try to introduce some of these elements into the scene. Be careful, though, not to cram something in that obtrudes. More important is your knowledge of the character's history. You don't need to make any of the traits or beliefs evident.

They could exist only in your mind. Now, with all ten elements in mind, tape the next scene.

EXERCISE 11: CHARACTER EXTENDED

> The same setting. The phone rings, and it is the clerk's mother.

                         CLERK
            Hotel Rex . . . Hi . . . It's
            three A.M. . . . What are you
            doing up? . . . Don't be silly.
            I'm fine . . . I'm telling you
            I'm fine. No . . . I'm studying.
            Got a final on Tuesday . . . No,
            I'm not taking pills . . . I
            know a lot of students do. I'm
            not . . . Yes. I drink coffee.
            No Mom. I don't drink that much.
            I know it's bad. . . . On Fri-
            day? Maybe. If I'm still alive .
            . . I was only joking. . . .
            Because this is the only job I
            can study on. We've had this
            discussion before . . . I know
            it's important. I know you're
            worried. Don't . . . Yes. . . .
            Yes. . . . I know. . . . I know.
            . . . Yes. Excuse me Mom,
            there's a guy pointing a pistol
            at my head . . . I think he
            wants a room. Wait! Don't call
            the police! (hits receiver) Mom?
            (hangs up) Merde!

                                              END OF SCENE

We now have the public self and the private self on tape. Are they the same person? View the scenes again. Does the public self show elements of the private one? We behave differently for different people and situations, but the actor mustn't change the primal elements of the character. Basically, this person has stayed the same from a very early age. The nuances of change should not be jarring. Though subtle variations give a character depth and interest, they can be achieved only when the actor creates a solid foundation.

Don't Wait for Magic

The critics are apt to say, "The actor hadn't found the character." The comment is usually caused by the actor looking for the character during performance. What the audience sees is a series of interesting vignettes, a schizophrenic rambling when the actor fails to achieve a coherent persona. Relying on the gods or the muses to find character almost always results in a performance where the character changes from scene to scene.

I can hear that stage actor yell from the back of the room, "What's wrong with that? It's kind of exciting!" Yes, there is a repertoire of plays wherein this method might be acceptable, plays whose characters are symbols or who live in a fashion far removed from normal psychological drives. But you are applying acting methods to film and television, and I assure you that avant garde is a rare animal in this world.

When you do plays you say to yourself . . . OK. I'm six feet tall, have dark hair, bad teeth, bunions, whatever. But every time I see myself on film, I think, Oh my God, that's all!

Annette Benning

If we accept that film creates a more credible reality than stage, it is logical to expect a very realistic character. You'll notice that I didn't say *truer*, because what is truer for stage or film has nothing to do with the comparative quality of either. They simply are different.

The actor on stage is never alone. Even in the most contemplative moments, the actor is aware of the audience. The good actor in film allows the camera to capture the most private moments without the audience ever being aware of the acting.

When people name their favorite movie, their choice is most often predicated on their memory of the characters. The characters motivate the plot, and not vice versa. This leads us to another way to help find the persona. Simply put, How do things that happen in the story affect your character, and how does your character affect the story? With all of the aforementioned techniques as guideline, you must now list the points in the story where even the most minute changes affect the character.

To become aware of this technique, let's begin with the character you should know best, yourself.

EXERCISE 12: YOUR DAY

This is not an acting exercise, but rather a way for you to be conscious of the changes you experience in your hour-to-hour living. Keep a journal for a day. In it, list every emotional event from the time you wake up until you go to sleep. Describe your feelings with short sentences. Nothing, absolutely nothing, should escape. For example:

"No parking spaces. I'll be late. If I'd gotten here earlier, I'd have a better chance of getting a space. I'm angry with those jerks who were here. I'm also angry with myself for not getting up earlier."

Videotape your reading of the journal. On playback, try to determine what attitude, if any, generally prevails. Look for the shifts between good feelings and negative ones. Make particular note of cause and effect. Are your responses what others would expect of you? Are they "normal?" It is very important that you not enhance your journal in an attempt to be more interesting. If the writing becomes literary, you are defeating the purpose of the exercise.

The next part of the exercise is to become a character of your choice, and write the character's journal. The character should be involved in pretty much the same activities as you—Don't let the character become involved in a murder mystery. Forget plot. Just let the character behave in normal, everyday circumstances. Videotape at least half an hour of yourself reading this character's journal.

Compare the "real you" journal tape to the invented character's tape.

We Are Known By the Things We Do

To play a person entirely different from yourself involves the same basic steps, only now your psychological tether is much longer. The question of how the character would react has no correlation to you in similar circumstances. It is a time for invention and discovery. Many actors enjoy the challenge because it allows them to go under the text and create that subworld where all interesting characters exist.

Unfortunately this is also the perfect opportunity to go overboard and make terrible choices, as stereotypes and prejudices rush to the foreground and display their comfortable wares to the innocent actor. I don't think there has ever been an actor who, at times, hasn't succumbed. What is most important is to keep a link, a thread, to your own reality.

For example: Anthony Hopkins' portrayal of Hannibal Lector, in *The Silence of the Lambs*. Here was a cannibalistic monster whose sense of humor gave him enough humanity to compel the audience to almost like him. It was that bit of Anthony Hopkins in there that made the character more complex, more human.

" . . . there was nothing new I would experience as a character that I had not already experienced as a 35 year-old . . . The one fundamental thing that I carry with me as an actor in every part I play is that at any moment, you are

re-creating. There is something you want. Once you know what, you just call on your memory bank and you've got it."

Sidney Poitier

Don't worry if the memory bank is only 18 years old. You'll undoubtedly play people your own age so use what's there and continue to make deposits.

The Dilemma

The creation of a unique character in a film and television presents an equally unique dilemma. Some very good actors who have succeeded in such a creation have found themselves repeating the role in film after film. A young leading man with a wide range of acting talent soon became a brand name by virtue of creating an indelible character. His name was Peter Lorre. In more recent films I think of Harry Dean Stanton, who seemingly cornered the market on the existentialist drifter.

So, how does this affect the actor contemplating a career in film? My conjecture is that habits are easily formed when the positive response to something you do is overwhelming. The desire to do it again is quite compelling. If you learn the right tricks, then see the incredible results, you certainly are tempted to use them again. Many actors have built careers and fortunes on such stuff and have won Academy Awards. Yet there is a very good reason to be cautious.

If you accept the fact that casting in film and television follows a realistic path, so that you will be cast according to age, type, and image, should you then develop yourself as a character? I think not. The difficulty becomes how to convince the people who cast you, because you are you, of the necessity to create a new persona: the character.

If you go too far, they might object with the rationale that they would have cast someone like that if they wanted such a person. The usual reason you were cast is that they saw your picture and were looking for someone like you. And yet, as a creative actor, you don't want the character to be just you.

In real life, we acquire manners, gestures, and attitudes that distinguish us from others. They are the habits that either endear us to people or stimulate more negative reactions. Many times I have heard people remark that when not performing, certain actors were quite dull; they were non-verbal and offered little to the social group. Elia Kazan said that Robert De Niro found release and fulfillment in becoming other people. If you have ever seen an interview with Mr. De Niro, you've recognized one of those actors who doesn't feel comfortable talking about himself or his technique.

Does this mean that you should repress your own personality to allow room for the character? I don't believe that's necessary. But I strongly caution you not to allow your personal idiosyncrasies to dominate role after role. This might lead to financial rewards, but could be very boring and frustrating artistically. The problem with this kind of success is that once it is achieved, it's very difficult to escape. (I know, you'll cry on the way to the bank.) The same problem faces actors in television series. Once the public becomes accustomed to an actor as a certain character, because of time and repetition, it is almost impossible for the actor to play other parts.

When you think about it, the same condition existed long before television. Two film stars come to mind: Jimmy Stewart and Bette Davis. In spite of their strong personalities, they both managed to become the characters in their films because of their equally strong talent. However, both impressed their images so indelibly on the public that no matter what role they played, there still remained a certain trademark effect.

The creation of character emanates from within, from meticulous study of details, minutia, body language, and voice. But two outside elements also contribute—costume and makeup. Whether you are an actor who works from the outside in, like Dirk Bogarde, or the opposite, (like method actors) or use any of the other techniques, makeup and costume will psychologically assist you.

Regardless of your technique, time, the nemesis of film and television acting, always raises its ugly head. Don't expect long, searching conversations with the director concerning the character. Read the script, do your homework, and bring something in. If you do this in an intelligent, methodical way, chances are you'll have something good.

> *Actors should make a choice. Even if they make the wrong choice it doesn't matter. You can change that, give them something else to play. They should decide the character's intention in the scene: that is what the character wants and how they intend to go about getting it. My approach is to work through actions . . . that is, every actor at every moment has an intention. The emotion is a byproduct.*
>
> *Glenn Jordan*

EXERCISE 13: CHOICES

Each character in the scene can be played in a variety of ways. Each couple should tape the scene at least twice, each time with new choices.

```
One enters and hands a piece of paper to Two. Two
reads the paper, then puts it down and looks at One.
```

                    ONE
Is there something wrong?

                    TWO
Maybe you should tell me that.

                    ONE
I don't know what you mean.

                    TWO
It is not the proper form. You
must use the proper form.

                    ONE
I'm sure it's the proper form
. . . I got it from the office.

                    TWO
The office?

                    ONE
You're the one who sent me
there.

                    TWO
No. I don't think so.

                    ONE
It was yesterday. I came to see
him and you told me that I
needed an entry permit. You sent
me to the office at the end of
the hall. I told them you sent
me and they gave me this.

                    TWO
They made a mistake if what
you're saying is true.

                    ONE
Of course it's true!

                    TWO
The point is that this is not
the correct form and you need
the correct form to see him. If

you get the correct form you can
see him next week on visiting
day.

> ONE
> Next week will be too late.

> TWO
> I see.

> ONE
> Please.

> TWO
> It isn't my fault you got the
> wrong form. You come in here and
> expect me to waive all of the
> procedures. I didn't bring the
> wrong form.

> ONE
> Two minutes . . . just two
> minutes. No one will know.

> TWO
> Leave.

> ONE
> To make it easier for you.

> TWO
> You cannot stay here. Leave.

One begins to leave.

> TWO
> If I let you in they would kill
> me.

> ONE
> I know . . . I'm sorry.

> TWO
> You come in asking for your
> favors because you love someone

and you don't think that you
could kill someone else if you
are obliged.

                    ONE
I'm truly sorry. Maybe I'll try
to get the proper form today.
Maybe they'll let me in for the
afternoon session.

                    TWO
No.

                    ONE
If I explain I got the wrong one
. . .

                    TWO
It wasn't wrong.

                    ONE
What did you say?

                    TWO
The form you brought was right.

                    ONE
But . . . I don't understand.
You said . . .

                    TWO
No matter what you brought, it
would be wrong. There is no
right form for you.

                    ONE
Why? Why this charade? You could
have told me this yesterday.
Damn you!

                    TWO
Quiet! I have already put myself
in enough danger by telling you
this. Now you must leave.
Please.

One starts out.

                    ONE
          I want to thank you.

One leaves.

                    TWO
          Thank you?

END OF SCENE

What does One want? How does One go about getting this? What does Two want? Where is the change, and how does it affect the characters?

Verbalize the subtext to the Group, and see if they recognized it in the performance. Does the body language reveal character?

It's been said there really is no such thing as character. Habitual behavior or action delineates what we are. The problem for the actor is in defining what that habitual behavior is. The philosophers and theorists of acting can call things what they want. The actor is the pragmatist who, from only the written word, must be able to bring someone to life. The film actor must be able to portray that life truthfully whenever the director says, "Action!"

Probably all married people in this world have heard this phrase from their spouses: "It's not what you said, it's the way you said it." To me this is a succinct definition of what the actor does to interpret a part. And like the married couple, you must live and react in the subtext. Then, and only then, do we see the behavior we call character.

Films to See

Marriage of Maria Braun: Directed by Rainer Werner Fassbinder. Hanna Schygulla's portrayal of a woman's rise to power is memorable.

Death in Venice: Directed by Luchino Visconti. Dirk Bogarde speaks very little dialogue in this slow-moving but fascinating film.

Dog Day Afternoon: Directed by Sydney Lumet. Al Pacino as a hoodlum, reveling in the spotlight.

Pele The Conqueror: Directed by Billie August. Max von Sydow won an Oscar nomination for his portrayal of Lasse Karlsson.

Thelma and Louise: Directed by Ridley Scott. Geena Davis and Susan Sarandon achieve a rare perfection in the connection of the two characters.

6

□ □ □
□ □ □
□ □ □

Focus

The Environment

Movie sets are busy places. Even when you are doing a very dramatic scene, you are aware of the camera moving, the microphone flipping back and forth to catch the dialogue, and all kinds of technical devices with people doing their jobs as you act. One flick of your eyelid that acknowledges any of this activity ruins the scene.

The actor must separate the brain into two parts. One part makes note of the technical requirements; the other ignores them completely and creates. When your focus throughout your performance is perfect, the audience loses you, the actor, and avidly accepts the character. It is then that the spectators cry, laugh, exalt, live, and die with the character you have created.

The Love Scene

There is nothing more difficult in film and television acting than the love scene. It is nearly always filmed in extreme closeup, involving complicated technical camera preparation because of that. To say that we all are most vulnerable in this kind of scene is an understatement. From puberty on, the idea of love, the ramifications of love, and most of all, the physical and psychological aspects of love, play a very important part in our lives.

Every so often you read of an actor who dismisses questions regarding love scenes with the casual remark, "All in a day's work." You may believe that, if the actor has made a lot of films with a lot of love scenes, but even then, I have serious doubts.

Let's forget the technical necessities and concentrate on the fact it's a love scene. The screen will show two large faces, inches away from each other, expressing some of the most personal human emotions. There on the set, inches from their lips, is a monster camera lens. Behind the lens are a camera operator, a director, a sound person holding a microphone 6 inches above them, and further back, about 30 more people in the crew.

All eyes focus on the actors. They are in bed, seminude. Each actor, without admitting it to the other, is extremely nervous. The director is nervous.

The words are clichés. How can they be otherwise? The camera can detect a lie in an instant.

It's a terrible situation. The actors are speaking tender words of love, and the audience could be laughing. The fact is, film and television love scenes are intimate, much more so than love scenes in plays. They're also difficult to perform, yet actors will put off rehearsing them fully until the camera is rolling. I'm not advocating sloppy wet kisses in rehearsal. But I am suggesting that the actors lie close together, in an embrace, faces an inch or so apart, to run lines before the scene is shot.

The actors will familiarize themselves with the situation this way so that when it comes time to shoot, they've gone through the nervous reactions and are ready to do the scene.

Because the filmed love scene demands reality, many of them are done nude or seminude. If this is the case, the actors should discuss their feelings about it and try to create a common bond regarding the situation. Let's face it, they're the only two people on the set without clothes. The actors should be reassured that great pains are taken to respect their propriety. In fact, I've never seen crews more unobtrusive than on the days this kind of scene is shot.

One hint for the actor: Use gum and mouth spray, and don't eat onions, garlic or spicy food before the scene. You hear stories about actors who violated this rule with relish.

EXERCISE 14: THE LOVE SCENE

Actors in each other's arms, very close. The camera and camera person should be as close as possible to get an extreme close shot of the actors' faces. Someone will play the director, another, the sound person, each within 3 feet of the actors. The rest of the class should also focus close attention on the actors. Yes, the idea is to make them as uncomfortable as possible. The scene must be played very slowly. The actors remain in one position.

ONE
```
I love you.
```

TWO
```
I love you too.
```

ONE
```
I love your smile.
```

TWO
```
I love your nose.
```

                    ONE
My nose?

                    TWO
And the way you talk.

                    ONE
You're crazy.

                    TWO
You love a crazy person.

                    ONE
I can't believe this happened to
us.

                    TWO
I knew it would.

                    ONE
You did?

                    TWO
It was Karma.

                    ONE
Karma?

                    TWO
You don't know what Karma is?

                    ONE
Uh-uh.

                    TWO
Well, Karma is. . . . I can't
believe you don't know this.

                    ONE
Hey, don't get mad.

                    TWO
I'm not mad . . . I'm just a
little amazed.

                    ONE
I love you.

```
A long pause.

                        ONE
           I really love you.

                        TWO
           I love you too.
```

END OF SCENE

I threw in the change of direction for fun. I'm sure there were enough giggles just getting into position. It's either that or getting very, very serious about the scene, with much discussion of where the hands go, whose nose is where, and solicitous questions about your fellow actor's comfort.

Love scenes are difficult on all levels. For the actor, the trouble is they evoke laughter if they aren't played well. You can succeed on a scale of 1 to 10 with any other kind of dramatic scene, but a love scene is either a 10 or a dismal failure.

The stage love scene can be quite poetic. The language in plays is often praised by critics and accepted by the audience, but something happens to those same lines when they are transformed to film. They become corny and theatrical. The film love scene uses naturalistic language, and, if the scene is written well, very little dialogue. Stage actors tell us their intimate thoughts; film actors (with a good script) keep quiet and show us.

> *I use the people I'm working with to generate emotion. In* Hat Full of Rain *I was supposed to be in love with Eva Marie Saint. I found there was so much of her that was easy to love, so I just used that. Then heightened it.*
>
> *Don Murray*

Some actors may have steamy on-screen romances and actually dislike each other in real life. I won't mention any names, but see *An Officer and a Gentleman* for example. It doesn't matter how you generate the emotion. It only matters that it's real. Unfortunately, many times the failed love scene is not an acting problem but a life problem. Actors may protect themselves from romantic love in their personal lives for various reasons. Unfortunately, such negative feelings are not easily disguised. The answer is to use any kind of love as your image—love of someone in your family, your best friend, your dog, your car . . . whatever—and use that image for your love scene. Substitution is a tried-and-true acting technique in all kinds of situations, and for the actor who has trouble with filming love scenes, it is one of the best solutions. In fact, for an experiment, you might try one of those non-romantic images when you do the love scene and see if anyone detects the substitution.

In any kind of scene, the problem with focus is that it can be easily faked. You could try an exercise where you read a dramatic scene while others tried to distract you, you would probably be able to continue without paying heed to any of the distractions. You would simply set your mind to your reading and resolutely ignore the distractions. But that is not dramatic focus.

Just as you can pretend to listen, you can also pretend to focus. For example, an actor at certain moments seems to be in the role, and then out of it at other moments. From scene to scene he shows fluctuations that have nothing to do with character development. Even within a scene, there seems to be no organic center, no continuity.

In all sorts of endeavors, athletic, academic, or artistic, you often hear someone say: "I can't understand it, I had it down so perfect at home. It was great at rehearsal or at practise." Athletes call it choking. "Whatever you call it, it happens to everyone at some time. The solution for actors is to recognize the symptoms and have a strong enough technique to overcome them.

Some actors, once they get into character for a movie, stay in that mode 24 hours a day. They eat, sleep and live the role. If they feel that is necessary, it certainly is their prerogative. I would rather the actors develop a method to call upon their characters at will and live the rest of their day-to-day existence as themselves. Pity the friends of an actor who lives the role of a serial killer!

To help you focus and correct this elusive acting fault, lack of focus, I have devised the following exercise.

EXERCISE 15: FOCUS

This exercise is in three parts and should be shot on three separate occasions, at least a day apart. The actors should not view the scene until all the segments have been taped. (It would be best if all segments were shot on the same tape.)

Part 1:

Actors One and Two sit side by side, close together, facing forward. They are admiring a view.

                    ONE
        I love this time of day.

                    TWO
        Yeah.

                    ONE
        Yeah?

                    TWO
          So . . . what's on your mind?

                    ONE
          I thought we came up here to
          admire the view.

                    TWO
          Oh.

                    ONE
          You always think there's some-
          thing behind everything.

                    TWO
          I'm paranoid. OK? Now that we've
          got that settled, let's just
          look at the view.

                    ONE
          Well, it's true isn't it?

                    TWO
          Whatever you say.

                    ONE
          It would be nice if you didn't
          patronize me.

                    TWO
          I didn't mean to. . . . The view
          is nice.

                    ONE
          OK.

                    TWO
          What do you want?

                                        END OF PART ONE

Part 2:

                    ONE
          I don't want anything?

                    TWO
Fine.

                    ONE
I say we admire the view.

                    TWO
Fine.

A long silence.

                    ONE
I know you lied to my father.

                    TWO
You can see the shoreline.

                    ONE
The question is why.

                    TWO
The waves breaking . . .

                    ONE
Why would you lie?

One looks at Two. Two turns to meet the gaze and
smiles.

END OF PART 2

Part 3

                    TWO
Is this a theory you have?

                    ONE
No. It's a feeling.

                    TWO
A feeling.

                    ONE
I know you.

> TWO

I see.

> ONE

Well?

> TWO

So you hiked me up this mountain
to inspire my confession.

> ONE

I'm your friend.

> TWO

Oh?

> ONE

I am.

> TWO

And you think I'm a liar.

> ONE

No.

> TWO

Yes you do.

> ONE

I thought you might like to tell
me.

Two turns away, looks at the view.

> TWO

When I was a kid, I used to
count the seconds between the
waves breaking. I think it
averaged about four seconds. . .
. (counts) One thousand. Two
thousand. Three thousand. Four .
. . I was right.

As Two begins counting again we see that One was
right about the lie. They both share the gravity of
the terrible secret.

                         TWO
One thousand. Two thousand.
Three thousand. Four thousand
. . . (Repeat if you wish.)

END OF SCENE

Upon completion of Part 3, view the three segments together.

Does the dramatic progression flow from part one to the next? Are the actors using the same voice levels? Inflections? Nuance? Does their mood give us a sense of place? Is it a hot summer morning or a brisk fall day? Do they make us see the view? Do we feel the connection between them throughout the sections? *Does the tape look as if it were shot in one long take?*

The process, then, is preparation (your homework) and focus, which I call the ability to deliver when called upon. The popular word for it is *charisma*. Some studio executives use the phrase, "The camera loves her or him." But I believe that what they are often describing is an actor in true focus—the person who compels you to watch.

For further focusing exercise, take any scene and break it up into three parts. Tape each part on a different day. Play them back together, and again look for that sense of continuity.

The one actor I nominate for perfection in both characterization and focus is Marlon Brando. View *A Streetcar Named Desire* or *On The Waterfront*. Look particularly for the scenes where Brando is listening and reacting.

EXERCISE 16: THE READING

Closeup. The actor looks to camera left, picks a spot, and holds.

                         ONE
I remember the place so well
. . . Even though I was only
five . . . You came around this
bend in the road and then suddenly you could see the village
and the small harbor. The fish-
ing boats were in . . . it was
late in the afternoon . . . A
few tourists were sitting at the
cafe. I always looked at them as
if they were tourists and I

```
wasn't. Sort of a superior me
against them. Anyway, it was my
village in a way. I bet none of
them had family from there. If
you looked up to the right of
the cafe and the flagpole you
could see where my grandparents
lived. There was a huge fig tree
in the courtyard and the roof
was slate blue. They died before
I ever got to know them. It was
so quiet there. Just the sounds
of the gulls and the boats
chugging in and out of the
harbor. You could smell the
fresh fish and the ocean in the
morning. Sometimes I thought I'd
like to live there. But I
didn't, did I? And I never went
back. I don't understand it. I
really don't.
```

END OF SCENE

To whom are you speaking?
Do you see the images?
Do we see them with you?
What is the speaker doing?

Imitation

A sure sign of wavering focus is imitation—a warning that belongs in all chapters. Beware of imitation. I don't mean imitating your favorite actor, I mean picking up the cadences and accents of the person you're acting with. Cadence or rhythm is the most insidious process. Cadence and imitation is a natural thing to do. As a scene progresses, you'll find that each person begins to respond in the same amount of time. In a fast-paced comedy scene, this may be fine. But it could be disconcerting in a dramatic scene, where symmetry could easily outweigh the meaning. American actors doing Shakespeare get into poetic grooves that may have the audience tapping their feet, at the same time wondering what they're saying.

Accents can be as dangerous. Because actors train their ears to pick up regional accents, they sometimes lapse into one without thinking. I know a lot of actors who, after spending a week in Texas or New York, sound as if they come from there. If you are in a scene with someone who has developed a mild accent, be aware of it, and make sure you are not mimicking them.

Focus stems from a feeling of confidence. Actors who are solid in their choices, intelligently and emotionally prepared, exude something extra, something undefinable, that compels us to watch. They are charismatic. Watching them makes us realize that acting is truly an art.

7

Comedy

The Big Difference

Drama has a forgiveness factor that allows it to partially fail yet have a certain measure of success. People may dislike certain scenes without having the whole event ruined for them.

Not so with comedy. It's a 10 or zero. If you don't get laughs, you don't have a comedy. My definition of acting hell is to be performing in play billed as a comedy, not get any laughs, and know there is another hour of play to go.

But let's look at a successful comedy. In theatre, the reaction is immediate, and the actors play off the audience reactions. Good comic actors learn from each performance and enhance their parts, finding laughs where there were none before.

Actors in film comedy have no such reactions to rely on. And even if the crew members wanted to react after seeing 10 rehearsals, they had better not ruin a take by laughing while cameras are rolling. No, acting in a comedy is serious business, where instinct, trust of the material, and the director play major parts in determining whether viewers find it funny.

Every year we read about someone we all accept as a serious actor saying she or he is tired of drama and wants to do a comedy. Some of these actors succeed and overcome the audience prejudice about their images, but a lot of them fail. Lousy script, bad director, horrible casting—their excuses are always the same.

You Need a Sense of Humor to Do Comedy

Have you ever met anyone who admits to having no sense of humor? People admit they have no ear for music. They even admit they hate dogs and children. But I have never heard anyone say, "I have no sense of humor."

The problem is defining what a sense of humor means. This is more difficult than it seems. When you try to analyze audience reaction at a play from night to night, you get a very confusing picture of what makes people laugh. One night they howl at every line; the next, deadly silence. Another time they laugh at all the wrong things. You'll notice I keep saying *they*. That is because audiences respond as a group, especially to comedy.

Many an actor has delivered a punch line (the one that always works), waited, and died through the silence, finally realizing *they* were not going to laugh. Then later in the play, the actor speaks a line that has never before even raised a chuckle. Wham! The audience stops the play with its roars.

It's been said that laughter is contagious. The opposite may also be true.

When you show a friend a cartoon you think is hilarious, and he hands it back without a smile, who's wrong?

So, if we can't even define a sense of humor, how do you know if you have one? If you think you don't, are you going to admit it? Most actors find out the hard way. They bomb in two or three comedies and make a vow to never do comedy again. But this might not be an intelligent way to make career decisions. Maybe the script was bad, the director was horrid, or. . . . Nevertheless, the stage actor has one advantage over the film and television actor. The verdict is swift and decisive.

The film and television actor won't find out whether or not the comedy works until months later when the picture is shown. If it's really awful, there's a chance it may become a cult classic.

You can learn techniques to alleviate the anxieties associated with performing comedy, but, as has been painfully shown in the past, there are no guaranteed results.

Comedy usually doesn't work if the actor thinks he's funny. Really lasting comedy is usually unconscious as far as the character is concerned. They don't think it's funny. You think it's funny. . . . In film, you cannot wait for the laugh because you're sure it's there. Nobody knows if it's there. You must play it legitimately. In Some Like It Hot *Billy Wilder gave one of the great pieces of direction in one of the greatest comedy scenes ever written. I had been out dancing with Joe E. Brown with a rose in my teeth and I'm lying in bed when Tony Curtis comes in from a date with Marilyn Monroe. I'm playing the maracas and he asks me what's up. I say I'm engaged. He says, "Congratulations, and who's the lucky girl!" Now I'm so psyched up about being a girl that I reply, "Me." Now after I say "engaged," Billy figured the dialogue would get buried with laughs, so in order to play the scene and hear the words, he devised a piece of business. I shook the maracas between lines and danced and sang like the happy girl I was. The spaces were filled with funny business, the scene held, and you could hear the dialogue. You have to look for a piece of business that is legitimate. In* Mr. Roberts *we had another*

kind of situation. When Ensign Pulver blows up the laundry and is covered
with soap lather . . . We shot the scene three different ways. First, we did it
like it was in the play, and I didn't wait for laughs. I filled in with blowing
soap bubbles and reacting to the stuff, and so on. We then did two other
versions. One a little slower and the next even slower. In other words, we
were giving the audience space to laugh. The last two versions bombed in
previews and we went back to the legitimate one. The audience may have
missed some lines, but it worked.

Jack Lemmon

I can think of many recent examples of the actor playing it straight and
letting the comedy happen. Leslie Neilson in *Naked Gun* thinks he's a mar-
velous detective. He is never aware of the mayhem he creates, nor does he
react to any of it. Very much like Inspector Clouzot (played by Peter Sellers)
in *Pink Panther*, he is intent on doing his job. If one were to take away the
sight gags and the terrible puns, Neilson could be acting in a corny police
drama.

John Cleese, in the TV show "Fawlty Towers," plays an apoplectic inn-
keeper who misunderstands almost every situation and bungles his way through
life. He is a man with a terrible disposition and a nagging wife. The humor lies
in the fact that Mr. Fawlty takes life very seriously and without knowing it
creates one crisis after the other. As things grow worse, they become funnier.
In *Ghost*, Whoopi Goldberg creates a more normal comic character; that is, if
one can count as normal a crooked, fake, medium who suddenly discovers her
powers are real.

Goldberg and Cleese are the sources of the humor, but in different ways.
We laugh *at* Basil Fawlty. We laugh *with* Whoopie. Even though the character
of Fawlty is exaggerated, Cleese plays him very seriously. In fact, it is the
intensity of the character that makes him so funny. This wild exaggeration is
missing with Goldberg and Neilson in their parts—they play them very straight,
very realistically.

Yet, if you watch closely, you'll see that both Whoopie and Leslie, even
though they play it legit, add a certain edge to their characters. I can describe
this edge only by saying it is evident that both of these actors have a good
sense of humor. It shows in their performances.

Now we're back to that phrase, *a good sense of humor.* Imagine Robert
Duval or Robert De Niro in Leslie Nielson's role. On a one-to-one basis with
their most intimate friends, these actors may be funny and witty, but their
personification, their *stamp*, makes it extremely difficult for the audience to
accept them as comedic actors.

You might think it the audience's fault. In some ways it is. Strong, dramatic actors will often by typecast by the public simply because of their

intensity, their talent, and a memorable part. One strong dramatic role will haunt them throughout their careers, and though they play a great variety of dramatic parts with full acceptance, as soon as they do a comedy, they are rejected in the most arbitrary fashion.

Sharing the blame with the public is the power structure of the film and television business. If you start out as an orange and are accepted as an orange, you work as an orange and are recognized as an orange. The moment you also want to be an apple, you may expect indignant cries of rejection.

The point is, you may be allowed a change or two very early on, but at some time, you, or someone, will decide whether or not you are a comic actor—one who can do comedy. Theatrical, film, and television history is full of comedic actors who have switched to drama and been accepted. The opposite is not so prevalent.

Don't Act Funny

I think the most boring thing in the world is to play results. If you play the laugh rather than the character, it never is funny.

Louise Latham

So, with all of the danger signals flying, let's attack the deadly business of comedy. But first we should agree to one basic rule. The comedy we're after is not falling-on-the-floor, gasping-for-breath humor. Let us be satisfied with the gentle smile, the audible sigh of recognition and perhaps a chuckle or two.

Your performance may reflect a radical change from the person you really are. A lot of people don't realize their comedic talent because they never search for it. You cannot tell whether actors can do comedy by their offstage persona. Two very funny actors come to mind, Woody Allen and Steve Martin. Both men, when not performing, are very quiet and shy, nothing like their stage persona. Even when both of them entertained in nightclubs and television doing stand-up comedy, their performances were in character.

Now is the time to unleash the demons of comedy that exist in your subconscious and to find a funny character.

EXERCISE 17: A WOMAN'S MONOLOGUE

As in the other exercises, you should create the character and subtext. But this time, try to give the person an edge, an odd way of looking at things, an honest, but not serious portrayal. You may use any business, props, or costumes that will help.

JANE

Let me tell you about Walter.
He's my third husband. Well,
technically he's my second and
third husband. The minister who
married us was sort of defrocked
about six months after the
ceremony. So Walter insisted we
marry again. This time we got a
judge. Walter felt that no
matter his morals, we'd still be
legal. Walter wants everything
to be just right. He craves for
things to be right. Not once in
our marriage has he failed to
mention, whenever a train is
late, that say what you want
about him, Mussolini got the
trains to run on time in Italy.
Then he always repeats *"Italy,"*
with his voice in the air signi-
fying a can-you-beat-that tone.
In the last few years, Walter
has stopped talking. He answers
all questions with grunts. At
meals he points to things when
he wants them. The only other
noise he makes is when he reads
the paper. Then he punctuates
the silence with occasional
"Hmms." I told him once he
sounded like a Buddhist monk,
and he asked me why. And when I
got lost trying to explain the
"Hmm" and the "ohm" sounds, he
turned to the sports page.
Walter is in the basement. He's
been there for three months.
He's fixing the water heater.
You may wonder how a person can
exist for three months without
food or water. But I don't
anymore.

EXERCISE 18: A MAN'S MONOLOGUE

SAM

Hon, can't we have to talk. Hey
. . . I can't talk to you when
you're washing dishes. Just sit
down. Good. No, I don't mind if
you iron. Just listen. I want to
tell you something. On the way
to work this morning, I ran a
stop light and somebody ran into
the car. Nobody was hurt. We got
a few hundred dollars in dam-
ages. The other car just scraped
the paint. Anyway, this cop
shows up and asks what happened
and I told the truth. Besides,
there were witnesses. So I get
cited for running the light and
we started to talking. It seems
we went to the same high school
in Chicago. Now here's the crazy
part. We were yakking away when
all of a sudden our eyes connect
and something clicked . . . Oh
no . . . No! I forgot to tell
you the cop was a lady. Well . .
. Hon . . . I don't like creases
in the sleeves. They look tacky.
Well, anyway I snapped out of it
and went to work. Then I go to
my usual taco stand for lunch
and there she is. The lady cop.
Hon, don't start the dishes . .
. please. Well, we finished
lunch and went to her place.
What are you doing? Hey! It's
very hard to talk over the
vacuum. Hon! Can you hear me?
This is kind of important. I
know it's weird and I can't
understand it. Please turn that
off! . . . Thanks. Where you
going? Forget the lawn. Hon,

aren't you going to say something? What do you mean, "hoo-
ray?"

END OF SCENE

After playback of each tape, the performer and the group should analyze what worked. Look for any point where something went wrong. Did the actor recover? Humor is so delicate that one rarely gets back all the way once a line goes sour.

Try to pinpoint the minute details that made the monologues funny or not. Was the business funny? Was the character a real person? Was the character likable in spite of the lines? It is a rare audience that thinks an unlikable character is funny. In spite of Basil Fawlty's many faults, he was still likable. Danny DeVito's character Louie De Palma in the TV show "Taxi" is another example of a rat you can't help liking.

Maybe a voice from the back of the room now complains, "I wasn't funny, because the script wasn't funny." That's a real possibility, and for that reason you should do a scene that critics, audiences, and actors have thought funny for years. Now whatever I choose, someone is not going to agree that it's funny. Such is the nature of the comic beast.

In the film and TV world, the actor's opinion in such matters doesn't count. If you audition and get the job, don't show up with a rewrite that sparks it up a bit. Just do it!

The same goes for the following scene. Just do it! And make it funny!

EXERCISE 19: *SOME LIKE IT HOT*

Joe and Sugar are at the beach. Joe has assumed the role of a very rich man to impress Sugar. The scene begins as she chases a beach ball and he trips her. As she falls, he lowers the *Wall Street Journal*.

JOE

Oh, I'm terrible sorry.

SUGAR

My fault.

JOE

You're not hurt, are you?

                    SUGAR
I don't think so.

                     JOE
I'd wish you'd make sure.

                    SUGAR
Why?

                     JOE
Because usually when people find
out who I am, they get themselves a wheelchair and a shy-
ster lawyer, and sue me for a
quarter of a million dollars.

                    SUGAR
Well, don't worry. I won't sue
you—no matter who you are.

                     JOE
Thank you.

                    SUGAR
Who *are* you?

                     JOE
Now really . . .

An offstage voice calls for her.

                     JOE
So long.

He begins to read the paper again. She throws the
ball back, then peers around the paper, studying
him.

                    SUGAR
Haven't I seen you some place
before?

                     JOE
Not very likely.

SUGAR
Are you staying at the hotel?

JOE
Not at all.

SUGAR
Your face is familiar.

JOE
Possible you saw it in a newspa-
per . . . or magazine . . .
Vanity Fair.

SUGAR
That must be it.

JOE
Would you mind moving just a
little? You're blocking my view.

SUGAR
Your view of what?

JOE
They run up a red and white flag
on the yacht when it's time for
cocktails.

SUGAR
You have a yacht?

She turns and looks seaward at a half-a-dozen yachts
of different sizes bobbing in the distance.

SUGAR
Which one is yours—the big one?

JOE
Certainly not. With all that
unrest in the world. I don't
think anybody should have a
yacht that sleeps more than
twelve.

                    SUGAR
          I quite agree. Tell me, who runs
          up that flag—your wife?

                    JOE
          No, my flag steward.

                    SUGAR
          And who mixes the cocktails—your
          wife?

                    JOE
          No, my cocktail steward. Look,
          if you're interested in whether
          I'm married or not—

                    SUGAR
          I'm not interested at all.

                    JOE
          Well, I'm not.

                    SUGAR
          That's very interesting.

Joe resumes reading the paper.

                    SUGAR
          How's the stock market?

                    JOE
          Up, up, up.

                    SUGAR
          I'll bet just while we were
          talking, you made like a hundred
          thousand dollars.

                    JOE
          Could be. Do you play the mar-
          ket?

                    SUGAR
          No—the ukelele. And I sing.

                    JOE
For your own amusement?

                    SUGAR
Well, a group of us are appear-
ing at the hotel. Sweet Sue and
Her Society Syncopators.

                    JOE
You're society girls?

                    SUGAR
Oh yes. Quite. You know—Vassar,
Bryn Mawr—We're only doing this
for a lark.

                    JOE
Syncopators—does that mean you
play that fast music—jazz?

                    SUGAR
Yeah. Real hot.

                    JOE
Oh. Well, I guess some like it
hot. But personally, I prefer
classical music.

                    SUGAR
So do I. As a matter of fact, I
spent three years at the
Sheboygan Conservatory of Music.

                    JOE
Good school! And your family
doesn't object to your career?

                    SUGAR
They do indeed. Daddy threatened
to cut me off without a cent,
but I don't care. It was such a
bore—coming out parties, cotillions—

                    JOE
Inauguration balls—

                    SUGAR
—opening of the opera—

                    JOE
—riding to hounds—

                    SUGAR
—and always the same Four Hundred.

                    JOE
You know, it's amazing we never
ran into each other before. I'm
sure I would have remembered
anyone as attractive as you.

                    SUGAR
You're very kind. I'll bet
you're also very gentle—and
helpless.

                    JOE
I beg your pardon?

                    SUGAR
You see, I have this theory
about men with glasses.

                    JOE
What theory?

                    SUGAR
Maybe I'll tell you when I know
you a little better. What are
you doing tonight?

                    JOE
Tonight?

                    SUGAR
I thought you might like to come
to the hotel and hear us play.

                    JOE
I'd like to—but it may be rather
difficult.

>   SUGAR
> Why?

>   JOE
> I only come ashore twice a day—
> when the tide goes out.

>   SUGAR
> Oh?

>   JOE
> It's on account of the shells.
> That's my hobby.

>   SUGAR
> You collect shells?

> Taking a handfull of shells from the pail.

>   JOE
> Yes. So did my father and my
> grandfather—we all had this
> passion for shells—that's why we
> named the oil company after it.

>   SUGAR
> Shell Oil?

>   JOE
> Please—no names. Just call me
> Junior.

END OF SCENE

Some Like It Hot. Screenplay by Billy Wilder and I.A.L. Diamond. Suggested by a story by R. Thoeren and M. Logan. Copyright 1959 Aston Productions Inc. All rights reserved. Released through United Artists Corp. By permission U.A. Corp. Billy Wilder, I.A.L. Diamond.

This scene could be called broad comedy. It is very close to skit comedy where the sense of reality is enhanced. Both Joe and Sugar are playing roles in the scene. That is, each is pretending to be something they're not. But the comedy from the scene depends on the actors delivering the lines seriously. That is, they should make no attempt to be funny. In the movie, Tony Curtis chose to do the scene as Cary Grant, while Marilyn Monroe played it innocent and awed. The problem with broad comedy is that if you go too far, the characters become cartoons and less credible.

In acting comedy you must try to maintain a certain charm, a warmth that allows the audience to recognize the genre, forgive the occasional excess, and participate with you in the fun. In short, you must enjoy the process and let it show.

Notice the wordplay spots in the scene that are tried-and-true comedy writing devices. Here is one:

SUGAR: I won't sue you no matter who you are.
JOE: Thanks.
SUGAR: Who are you?

This requires precise timing to get the complete reversal. At another wordplay spot, Sugar complains of boring parties and cotillions and Joe replies, "inauguration balls." The writers use this device again when Sugar is trying to find out whether or not Joe is married. This demands a quick rhythm where they each seem to be caught up in a kind of doggerel. Look for these writing tricks in broad comedy scenes. You must also make various choices throughout the scene. That is, don't rely on the lines for the humor, but look for a variety of feelings, which, in turn, will influence your delivery. *A comedy character can be just as complex as a dramatic one.*

The next exercise is more subtle, less funny, and easier to play. The previous scene needs laughs to make it succeed. The following scene, less broad, will settle for knowing grins.

EXERCISE 20: SUNDAY

One enters. Two is reading the paper.

                    ONE
        I just love Sunday.

                    TWO
        Yeah.

                    ONE
        Did you hear me?

                    TWO
        You love Sunday.

                    ONE
        I can tell by the sound of your
        voice that you do too.

A long silence.

                    ONE
          I don't see what's so terribly
          wrong about saying that I love
          Sunday.

                    TWO
          I didn't say it was wrong. Can
          you manage to love Sunday with-
          out making a big deal out of it.

                    ONE
          I'm not making any big deal out
          of it. I would just like a
          response when I say something.

                    TWO
          Response? Who are you talking
          to. Response? Is this the gas
          company representative? Your
          response to the letter of the
          fifth was . . .

                    ONE
          Shut up!

                    TWO
          Let me read the paper and you'll
          not hear another word.

A long silence.

                    ONE
          I like Sundays. I prefer Sundays
          when it rains or snows. I like
          to make a bowl of chili and look
          out the window. Maybe build a
          fire . . .

A look from Two.

                    ONE
          Definitely build a fire.

               TWO
Prefer? Did you say prefer?

               ONE
I may have . . . It's a word
that I may use. I know the word.
Let's, for argument sake, and
I'm sure that's a condition you
most enjoy, let's just say that
I said "prefer." In fact, now
that you mention it, I did say
"prefer." Your response was
correct . . . I said "prefer."

               TWO
You talk like a professional
service person. *"Response."*
"Prefer." They're prissy little
words.

               ONE
"Prissy" is a prissy little
word.

               TWO
It's one you don't hear from an
AT&T operator. I talk like a
human being, not a robot.

A silence.

               TWO
I'm sorry.

               ONE
Yeah?

               TWO
I am . . . No excuses.

               ONE
It takes so little to set you
off.

                    TWO
You push the right buttons.

                    ONE
So it's my fault.

                    TWO
No.

                    ONE
No means *yes*.

                    TWO
No means *no*.

                    ONE
I prefer your response to be
truthful.

                    TWO
Let's forget it. Please?

                    ONE
OK.

                    TWO
Actually, I love Sunday too.

                    ONE
Don't just say that to make me
feel good.

                    TWO
If I said I love the frigging
day I meant that I love it.
Don't be telling me what I love
and what I don't love. Accept
it. I love Sunday. It's very
important for you to believe it
when I say that I love Sunday. I
love it! I love it.

                    ONE
Not when you say it like that!

<pre>
                    TWO
          It's the content that counts.
          Not how I say it. Besides, I
          said it with all my heart and
          soul. Now let's read the Sunday
          paper and shut up before I
          change my mind.

A long silence.

                    ONE
          I think it's about to rain.

                    TWO
          You're right.

                    ONE
          How about a bowl of chili?

                    TWO
          Sounds good.
</pre>

END OF SCENE

The *Some Like It Hot* scene could never play as drama. "Sunday" can. What are the main elements of humor in the scene? Could it be the absurdity of the argument? If you treated the argument as a symbol of deeper emotions between the two, I think you'd have a very unfunny scene. But if you just accept the scene for what it is, a silly argument between two rational people, it may play as comedy.

The problem with comedy scenes on playback is that after you've viewed the second or third version, the reactions begin to fizzle. The same thing happens on the set as you perform the scene a dozen times. By the twelfth time, the edge is gone, and you panic. This usually triggers a dangerous response, from the actor—He makes radical changes in choices, new, broader business. Mugging. Ad libbing. Playing to the camera instead of the other actor. *All Deadly.*

You must trust the material. Of course, on repeated takes you should find fresh ideas, nuances, and small variations. But I caution you not to mistake normal feelings of losing the humor and overreact. If the material worked the first and second times, chances are it will still work on Take 11.

The key to comedy acting is credibility. You must not think that you as the character are funny. Look at *Some Like It Hot*. Jack Lemmon, as the character, truly believed that he was a woman and engaged to a very rich man. His exuberance, coupled with Tony Curtis's disbelief, made the scene hilarious. If, for a moment, Lemmon's character had revealed that it was a put-on, the scene would have failed.

Films

Some Like It Hot: Directed by Billy Wilder. Ensemble comedy at its best. This is broad comedy with slight gags and jokes. Once the tone is set, the audience accepts the incredible happenings and sits back to enjoy itself.

Bringing Up Baby: Directed by Howard Hawks. Sophisticated comedy deftly done by Cary Grant and Katherine Hepburn. Note the restaurant scene where she rips her dress. Terrific blocking and business. Who says you can't have a touch of slapstick in sophisticated comedy?

All of Me: Directed by Carl Reiner. Steve Martin's struggle with himself is a little broader comedy than you see in the other films mentioned, but a great example of comedic body language.

TV Show

"Monty Python": From the ridiculous to the silly, the whole troupe performs the sketches with serious fervor. Quite often they parody an officious government or business type, or make comment on the modern human condition. But, no matter how broad, they are very character-orientated.

8 Situation Comedy

History

From vaudeville, burlesque, stage reviews, and some musicals, a style of acting emerged called sketch comedy. A sketch was a short piece of material, usually no more than 7 or 8 minutes. The actors portrayed broad stereotypes. They waited for the laughs, took pies in the face, did pratfalls, and played directly to the audience. Nothing was taboo. The best sketch comics went on to become major television stars in the infancy of television, when variety shows were popular. Such comedians as Jimmy Durante, Eddie Cantor, and Ed Wynn were some of the first people to headline their own TV shows.

Later a show called "Laugh In" featured this kind of comedy. After that, "Saturday Nite Live" and "Monty Python" carried on the tradition. But the single most important offspring of this sketch brand of humor is the situation comedy, known as sitcom.

In situation comedy, continuing characters do a *book* show: that is, a show with a story line. Because situation comedies are a major source of employment, it's a good idea to examine how they work from the actor's point of view.

If there is one word to describe the difference between acting for situation comedy and acting for film and television comedy in long form (movies, teleplays), I nominate *exaggeration*. In chapter 7 on comedy, I suggested giving an edge to the character. In sitcom, you can give it two edges and not be afraid of going over.

Every sitcom character is a bit of a caricature. On the "Mary Tyler Moore" show, the actress of that name played a young woman, Mary Richards, who worked in a TV newsroom as a co-producer of the nightly news, lived in a nice apartment, and had "real" problems. Her boss, Mr. Grant, played by Ed Asner, was the news director. His job was to get the news on the air and to manage the diverse group of newsroom employees. These two were by far the straightest, most normal characters on the show. But neither of them would have put up with Ted Baxter, the egocentric anchorman, for a moment, if they had played it realistically.

The Ted Baxter character (played by Ted Knight) necessitated some acting adjustments by Mary and Mr. Grant. The newsroom became sort of a newsroom, but more like a theatrical set, with desks and typewriters as props. On this set Mary and Mr. Grant interacted with the other people in the cast, who either set up or participated in the jokes. Though the jokes emanated from our knowledge of their characters, you can be sure they were jokes.

The scripts were carefully crafted so the laughs would come with precise regularity. The general rule is three or four jokes a page, which means three or four jokes a minute. To assure the success of this formula, the producers reinforce the studio audience's reactions with a laugh track.

It is essential for the actor to realize this for one reason—*the pace of sitcom acting is regulated by the number of jokes on the page.*

A Unique Arena

In drama or straight comedy, by virtue of the script, you can prepare and deliver lines without regard to external ideas of pace. You create an inner logic that allows the viewer to participate with you in your thought process. In the preceding chapter on comedy, I warned you not to wait for the laughs, because there was no guarantee they would come. Not so with the sitcom.

You wait. Because if there is even a glimmer of a laugh, you can be sure that it will be augmented in edit. Lines are not allowed to die. This practice is much abused. Too often a character says hello and gets a huge laugh.

Most sitcoms are done in front of a live audience. (This is usually announced on the air so the viewer, I suppose, won't think it a dead audience.) The reason is that the actors can measure their performance by the reactions of the audience. They tape two performances, one they call the *dress* and the other the taped show. Editors then cut these two performances together for the aired version.

Sitcoms always use multiple camera techniques. One camera is on the master, or long shot. Two other cameras cover the over-the-shoulder closeups. A fourth camera may just isolate the star. This multiple camera setup makes it imperative for the actors to hit their marks. If you're off by half a foot, you could be covering another actor's closeup.

The more successful shows rely on our familiarity with the characters to get their laughs. Thus, the jokes are based on prejudicial knowledge. The worst shows go for gags just for their own sake. Here, let's deal with acting for the shows that are well-written, clever, and character-orientated.

Your Bit Part on "Cheers"

"Cheers," one of the most successful shows in the history of television, has a cast of characters well-imbedded in the American TV psyche. An episode comes up where the bar sink is stopped up and they need an actor to play a plumber, a five-line part. The situation is that it's the plumber's first job, and he or she is very nervous. Sam Malone, played by Ted Danson, notices the plumber's shaking hands. The rest of the formidable cast is also present, all making comments and offering advice.

You're in the midst of people who have done show after show for 5 years. It's time for you to read for the part. What do you do?

1. You are not playing a plumber—you are playing an idea of what a plumber is. You need not do any research as to what plumbers really do in such a situation. In fact, it's best not to know anything about plumbing at all.

2. With absolutely no skill or knowledge, your intention is to fix the sink.

3. You do not want anyone to know this is your first plumbing job and that you are extremely nervous. (You also might not want them to know it's your first sitcom job.)

4. Use the fact that the cast all know each other and you are an outsider. (Make your nerves work for you.)

5. Make the plumber a *character* in a sitcom. That means you exaggerate the walk, the talk, the use of props.

    When you read for any part in a sitcom, don't be afraid to exaggerate. Not doing enough will seldom get you hired. Directors like the idea that you're willing to let it all hang out.

6. Know the show. A plumber on "Cheers" is different from a plumber on "Roseanne." You must carefully analyze the comedy style of the show and gear your performance to that style. For instance, on "Roseanne," the star, Roseanne Barr, gets most of the jokes. The other characters play straight: they set up the situation for the punch line. On "Cheers," the whole cast has punch lines at one time or another. That ensemble feeling can also apply to the bit player coming in for one scene.

7. One last important note: However you can, find out about the star's idiosyncracies, working habits, and peeves. Sitcom filming involves a lot of pressure. Lines are changed constantly. Ratings may be down that week, so the network executives are lurking around, making the star nervous. The point is that something as simple as watching a scene from the sidelines and being in the line of sight of the performing star could get you fired.

EXERCISE 21: SITCOM SCENE

This scene from "Cheers" with Rebecca and Sam needs no explanation. Try to play it with a fresh approach. Don't emulate the show.

Interior of Rebecca's apartment. Night.

It's late. The drapes are closed and the only light comes from a table lamp. In the dim light we see Rebecca, in a stupor, sitting alone on the couch. She wears a ratty bathrobe and slippers. She has a drink in her hand. Around her are empty liquor bottles, filled ashtrays, dirty dishes and empty pizza boxes. The place is trashed and so is she. We hear the sound of the doorbell; it jolts her. She moves unsteadily to answer it.

> REBECCA
> Hold your horses, I'm just
> putting down my beverage. Here I
> come.

She opens the door, concealing herself behind it.

> REBECCA (CONT'D)
> Ow!

SHE TALKS TO SAM THROUGH A CRACK IN THE DOOR.

> REBECCA (CONT'D)
> Hey, you're not the pizza boy.
> But you're still cute. Come on
> in.

Sam enters the apartment. Because it's dark he walks right into a table.

> SAM
> Ow! How can you see anything in
> here?

> REBECCA
> I'll just open the drapes and
> let some light in here, okay?

She starts for the window, but is so unsteady she lands back on the couch.

> SAM
> Let me just get a lamp.

Sam turns a lamp on. She turns it off. He turns it on again. She turns it off.

> SAM
>
> "Click."

Rebecca turns the lamp on. The light causes her to blink in confusion.

> SAM
>
> Sweetheart, you're not getting your security deposit back on this place.

> REBECCA
>
> Come on, Sam, sit down and join me in a toast.

Sam crosses back to the couch.

> SAM
>
> Rebecca, are you drinking again?

> REBECCA
>
> I certainly am not. I never stopped. (Puts down the glass) There, I stopped. (Picks it up) Now I'm drinking again.

> SAM
>
> Rebecca, if something's bother-ing you, you can't use alcohol to forget it.

> REBECCA
>
> Sure I can. I've forgotten everything that's happened in the past two minutes. (Then) Hey, you're not the pizza boy. But you're cute.

She tries to take another drink. Sam grabs the glass out of her hand.

> SAM
>
> Give me that.

He also scoops up as many other glasses and bottles
as he can carry.

                    REBECCA
          Sam, you don't have to clean up.
          I just did.

                    SAM
          It's okay. I'll just put them in
          the kitchen.

Sam crosses to the kitchen.

                    SAM
          (Re Glasses) Hey, these glasses
          are from the bar.

Sam exits into the kitchen. Once he's gone, Rebecca
goes back to the couch, sits down, and notices that
she's caught her hair with the end of her cigarette.
She stamps it out. Sam reenters and joins Rebecca on
the couch.

                    REBECCA
          Well, look who's back.

                    SAM
          Look, Rebecca, do you want to
          talk? Does all of this have
          something to do with your get-
          ting married? Are you starting
          to get cold feet?

                    REBECCA
          No. I'm perfectly prepared to
          marry Robin and spend the rest
          of my life with him. I'm just
          not particularly looking forward
          to it.

                    SAM
          What do you mean? All you've
          done for the last two years is
          talk about marrying this guy.

                    REBECCA
          Well, Sam, it's one thing to

love somebody while they're
serving time for you. But it's
another when you're serving time
with them. I mean, there's so
much of life I still haven't
tasted. After all, I've just
discovered this drinking thing.

                SAM
Sweetheart, I understand the
temptation. After all, I am a
recovering alcoholic.

                REBECCA
I just don't think I'm ready to
make a commitment.

                SAM
Hey, doubt is part of every
relationship. I should know. I
was divorced.

                REBECCA
I drink for a couple of days,
you were an alcoholic. I'm
having a little trouble with a
relationship, you were divorced.
Do you retain water in the
middle of the month, too, Sam?

                SAM
I'm just trying to help you.
Listen, everybody gets cold feet
before their wedding. But it's a
pretty weenie reason to turn to
alcohol.

                REBECCA
Why did you start drinking, Sam?

                SAM
I lost my curve ball.

                REBECCA
I'm not drinking because I've
got cold feet. I'm drinking

because I don't know if I love
Robin.

                SAM
Oh, wow. You think you don't?

              REBECCA
I just don't know. I just wish I
had more time to decide what to
do. Do you think there's any
chance the parole board would
keep him in prison for a little
while longer?

                SAM
Rebecca, if you don't love
Robin, why don't you just back
out?

              REBECCA
It's that easy? I'm supposed to
tell the richest man in the
world I don't want to marry him?

                SAM
He's not rich anymore, remember?

              REBECCA
In that case, what's his number?

                SAM
Come on Rebecca, this is serious.

              REBECCA
It's just that I keep remember-
ing that one time in my life I
had something so much more
exciting.

                SAM
Oh-boy. I think I know where
this is going.

              REBECCA
Oh, God, I loved it so much,

Sam. I think about it all the
time. It was so magical, so
thrilling.

                SAM
I know. I know.

            REBECCA
It was like every nerve ending
in my body was alive. Like my
skin was glowing. I was totally
at one with another being. Once
that happens to you, you never
forget it.

                SAM
Yeah, I'll never forget the
night we made love.

            REBECCA
No. I'm talking about when I was
ten and won first place in the
horse show. (Realizing) But that
night with you was good, too.
See, even sleeping with you was
better than Robin.

                SAM
Even that.

            REBECCA
So that's it . . . I don't want
to marry Robin. It's over. Well,
I guess I won't need this anymore. (Pulls a bottle out from
under a lamp) I've made my
decision. Robin is history. That
feels good. Let's celebrate.

She reaches for the bottle again. Sam grabs it.

                SAM
That's enough of that.

            REBECCA
You're right, Sam. There's a

> better way to celebrate. Drop
> your pants.

                    SAM

> What?

                 REBECCA

> You heard me. I want you.

                    SAM

> Whoa, hold on. We can't do this,
> Rebecca.

                 REBECCA

> Sure we can. Come on, Sam, the
> train is leaving the station.
> All aboard. (Makes train noises)

Sam slides away from her, but she follows.

                    SAM

> I won't do this, Rebecca.

                 REBECCA

> Why not Sam?

                    SAM

> First of all, you've been drink-
> ing, and gentlemen have rules
> about that. And second of all,
> you're repulsive right now.

                 REBECCA

> Can't take it?

                    SAM

> I'm getting out of here.

                 REBECCA

> What's your hurry? (Singing)
> "We've got tonight . . . Who
> needs tomorrow   . . ."

                    SAM

> Oh, no. No, honey.

REBECCA
(Screeching the high notes)

"Let's make it last, babe . . .
Let's FIII-ND a way . . ."

Rebecca has backed Sam against the wall.

REBECCA
Sam Malone, get ready for the
wildest night of your li-i . . .

She faints forward into Sam's arms. They slide to
the floor.

SAM
(Pinned under her) Oh, well,
gee, maybe I'd be more in the
mood if we washed your hair.

END OF SCENE

This scene, besides being difficult as comedy, has one of the hardest jobs in acting—portraying the drunk. If you ever have a chance of going overboard, getting corny, and being just plain awful, it's when you face the challenge of playing drunk. One of the clues to this difficulty is trying to do too much at the same time.

Drunks stagger, they slur their speech, they blink their eyes, they lose their train of thought; drunks have a variety of characteristics that occur or stop without reason. To play a drunk, I think the actor should choose one predominant behavior and then season it sporadically with other impairments. Then you should just imagine these problems and work them ever so faintly into the fabric of the character as the person would behave when sober. In other words, don't act generically drunk, be drunk as the character would be. From that point you may exaggerate a bit, and just a bit.

Suppose you decide on slurring words. Drunks hear themselves speaking naturally. Pick a sentence from the script. Take two words from the sentence, (words with similar consonants) and make them your key slur words. These are the words you'll come close to saying correctly. Pick two other words in another speech, and so on. If two don't work, pick three or four. The idea is to build on behavior, slowly.

Because it is a comedy, you still have to give this scene an edge. The fact is, a drunk in today's society is thought of as a sick and tragic figure. Whereas drunks used to be used as comedy relief in films, modern thinking people no longer find that condition, in itself, amusing. Even in this scene, Rebecca does have a genuine problem, but it would be a mistake to play it so real as to kill the humor.

Although humor quite often reflects very serious situations, it's the comedy actor's job to play the humor and leave the serious undercurrent to the viewer. Many sitcoms touch on serious issues, but they do it with a lot of laughs. If they didn't, they wouldn't be called sitcoms.

The last point about this very special milieu is to not get any snobbish attitudes. Sitcoms are not beneath your talents. All of your classical training has not gone to the dogs. Your parents and friends will not disown you. Your fellow thespians will probably envy you.

Sitcom acting can be a demanding and highly skilled technique. If you give it the same attention as any of the other disciplines of acting, it will be very rewarding.

Sitcoms to Watch

"I Love Lucy"
"The Honeymooners"
"All In the Family"
"The Cosby Show"
"Cheers"
"The Mary Tyler Moore Show"
"Murphy Brown"
"Coach"

9 □□□
□□□
□□□

The Closeup

Of all the techniques I've mentioned, the closeup is the only one that is wholly unique to film and television. I don't know who said, "the camera never lies," but that person is almost right. I say "almost" because it is possible to fool the camera. Many politicians will attest to that (in private). But actors would be wise to believe the phrase. Because the closeup shot can be the singularly most important tool, it can also be the most damaging.

Diane Ackerman wrote in an article in the *New York Times*:

There is a code of basic facial expressions that all humans share—happiness, anger, fear, surprise, disgust. Spontaneous, automatic, the face forms words before the mind can think them. We often rely on facial semaphore to tell us truths too subtle or shameful or awkward or intimate or emotionally charged or nameless to speak.

" . . . *The face forms words before the mind can think them.*" What a provocative idea! It suggests that we react first on a primal level, then think. Heroes who rescue babies by diving into raging waters invariably say, "I didn't have time to think."

Of course to react purely in such a way is impossible while acting. From the text you know the words and the emotions, and though there may be some surprises in performance, they are most always in the context of the scene. No one wants to act with someone who leaves the script whenever the mood hits her; yet there is a sense of danger when fresh emotional things happen and the scene breathes a life it never had before.

It's like the fast break in basketball, where three players pass the ball back and forth with precision, and the last one shoots the basket. None of them knows when the ball is coming, yet, when they get it, they respond perfectly, and in so doing become part of the event which culminates with scoring a basket. They clap hands together and smile at their accomplishment.

The fast break is a product of training, imaging (knowing how it's supposed to look), and instinct. It is never the same, but always has the same goal. Each player responds spontaneously within the circumscribed rules.

Acting should be that organic.

Let us divide the closeup shot into two main categories—realization and change of direction.

Realization

Films and television use the closeup to tell us important facts about character and plot. Oftentimes, wordless moments occur when the character realizes something and changes because of it. This might not be a distinctive acting problem for stage, but it certainly is for the camera. The film director isolates those moments in closeup, thereby creating a unique acting problem.

EXERCISE 22: REALIZATION

This is the time in the story where things begin to add up, the place where instincts and gut feelings take over. During realization words and logic have no meaning. The character faces unbearable truths, or the sky clears and the sun shines.

Before taping, mark the points in the script where you intend to change.

Camera is on the listener in a closeup. The speaker is off camera. The scene should be taped without the rest of the group watching.

> **VOICE**
> I'm glad you came. I've been
> meaning to talk to you for a
> couple of weeks, but you know
> how busy we get at Christmas . .
> . . You're looking great . . .
> you always do. Well, I only have
> a minute. The damn store is
> packed and we can't get any good
> help. Hell, that's not your
> problem . . . . Like I said I
> was meaning to call but . . . .
> I know we made some plans for
> the holiday . . . what I didn't
> know at the time was that my ex
> was coming to town. I didn't
> expect it. She's/he's visiting
> her/his mom and . . . It's a
> family situation. I just don't

```
think you'd feel comfortable.
You know I want to be with you .
. . it's just . . . You know . .
. they're all sentimental about
Christmas and how it used to be.
You OK? . . . I knew you'd
understand . . . I'll call. Hey,
I'd hate to put in that spot . .
. I knew you'd understand. We
still have New Year's Eve. I'll
call . . . . I promise.
```

END OF SCENE

Does the tape version match the points you indicated on the script? Does the realization take time to build, or do you reach the climax too early, leaving yourself nowhere to go at the end? Are you frustrated, angry, disappointed? Have you resolved never to see this person again, or will you forgive? What kind of person would do this to you? Does your response correlate to that person's behavior?

EXERCISE 23: LOVE REALIZED IN CLOSEUP

Again, the camera is on the listener. Someone you know and have loved has come back after a long time. The person in the past has not realized your love, but now you see that times have changed.

> **VOICE**
> I know you must think that I'm
> stupid. You must have wondered
> what I was doing, going here and
> there, never making up my mind
> about what I wanted. The years
> seem wasted, but then I don't
> know how it could have been
> different. I wasn't such a good
> risk then . . . I can't even
> guarantee that now. But I do
> know this . . . for all the
> years, no matter what I did or
> where I was, I never stopped
> thinking of you. I loved you

```
then and I love you know. And I
don't blame you if you tell me
to go to hell. But I want you to
know there'll never be another.
I want you to know that I'll
love you and only you until the
day I die.
```

END OF SCENE

Note the emotional stepping stones that take you from friendly under-standing to the realization that you are loved.

Change of Direction

Whereas realization is mostly a gradual process, the change of direction can be either gradual or abrupt, though the dramatic process usually makes an abrupt change of direction more interesting. The writer utilizes this device to stimulate the audience and to stay one step ahead of them. If dramatic writing were to follow a rigid path based on pure logic, we'd have some boring movies and TV shows.

The unexplained complexities of human nature allow the writer to break a character away from what seems an inexorable path and thus send the story off into new, exciting directions.

It is a lucky actor whose character is the instrument of such change. It is the dumb actor who makes change-of-direction choices when the text doesn't call for them. The snappy phrase for such behavior is "going against the text." Most of the time, this is an attention-getting device instigated by lack of real preparation and respect for the other actors and the script. The rare times this works are also dangerous, because it may encourage the actor to try it again.

Changing direction is not an arbitrary way to alleviate boredom or to have fun, but a legitimate acting technique you should use only when the text calls for it.

EXERCISE 24: CHANGING DIRECTION

This is a Parent/Student scene. Camera focus closeup on the Student.

PARENT
You packed?

```
                STUDENT
You know I've been packed for
days.


                PARENT
You nervous?


                STUDENT
A little. Hey, don't forget that
check.


                PARENT
I won't. I'll send it to the
dorm.


                STUDENT
I can get a job.


                PARENT
I want your first year to be
smooth . . . After that you'd
better get a job because I'm
going to be broke. I remember
the first day I went away to
university.


                STUDENT
You know . . . I really appreci-
ate what you're doing for me.


                PARENT
I know.


                STUDENT
Sometimes you might think that I
act like I don't. I know I drove
you a little bit crazy this
year.


                PARENT
What you're doing now made it
all worth while. I'm proud of
you.


The phone rings and the student answers.
```

                  STUDENT

Hey . . . what's shaking? What?
Fantastic. No . . . I'm about
ready to leave. No . . . I made
up my mind . . . I'll call. Hey,
don't forget your old friends
. . . I'm really jazzed for you
guys . . . Later.

Student hangs up, waits a beat, then returns to
Parent.

                  PARENT
What was that all about?

                  STUDENT
We got a record contract . . . I
mean the band got a contract.

                  PARENT
That's wonderful.

                  STUDENT
Yeah. Let's go.

Student picks up bag, heads for door, then stops.

                  PARENT
What did you forget?

A long pause.

                  STUDENT
Me. I almost forgot me.

                  PARENT
What do you mean?

                  STUDENT
It means I'm not going.

                  PARENT
It's a little late now to be
saying that. . . . So the band
got a record contract. There'll

be other bands . . . after you
graduate.

                STUDENT
I'm not going because of you. I
love you a lot, but I can't do
this you . . . I thought I
could. I almost convinced myself
that this is what I wanted . . .
maybe I will someday. But not
now . . . I'm going to play
music. It's something I really
want to do . . . I'm sorry.

Student goes to phone and dials.

                STUDENT
Hey Chris . . . I changed my
mind. I'm not going. You haven't
found a guitar player yet, have
you? . . . . Great!

                                    END OF SCENE

Change-of-direction scenes like this one are mostly based on the character's repression of what he or she really wants. This repression manifests itself as tension. The pleasant facade of the Student in the preceding scene masks this repression. But the actor must be careful that the facade itself is not so obvious that the audience is counting the seconds to the eruption. The Student can also choose to be somewhat hostile, although the character expresses love for the Parent.

The Parent seems to have won a long, hard-fought battle, only to be defeated at the last moment. The Student can make several choices about how to acknowledge that. The Parent begins to *realize* as the Student talks on the phone.

I think it would be interesting to play the scene with a lot of tenderness and love, and then repeat it with a more hostile edge from both people.

Find other realization and change-of-direction scenes, and tape them in a similar way.

Films

The Magnificent Ambersons: Directed by Orson Welles. The last scene with Joseph Cotton and Agnes Moorhead is a fine example of realization.

The 400 Blows: Directed by Francois Truffaut. The young boy never really escapes his repressive life. The last scene does offer some relief from the inexorable tension. The freeze frame is so real, so poignant, you can't believe this is a movie.

Suspicion and *Rebecca:* Directed by Alfred Hitchcock. Both films illustrate a woman in emotional jeopardy, frightened, repressed. Both use the woman's emotional change at the end as their main plot point.

It's a Wonderful Life: Directed by Frank Capra. Jimmy Stewart's last scene is still one of the greatest realization scenes on film.

10

□ □ □
□ □ □
□ □ □

The Workplace

The Set

A movie stage is a small country run by a benevolent, enlightened (we hope) dictator called the director. It is designed for efficiency in making the film and little else. The back of the set faces bare walls with thick soundproof material. Electrical and grip equipment is stored along the edges. It is a large warehouse, an esthetic horror, and not very comfortable.

In the middle of this space is the set. Above it is a grid where large lights are hung. The sound cart with its tape recorder and perhaps a few chairs line the perimeter. On a shooting day, the set is always crowded with people doing their various things—gaffers, grips, boom person, property person, set designer, makeup artist, camera crew, production assistants—all necessary for the scene that's to be shot.

In most production centers, these jobs are unionized. This only means one important thing to the actor. If something on the set needs to be moved, and it is not during a scene, don't move it. You are there to act and not be "helpful" by infringing on someone else's job. This also applies to non-union sets.

In a far corner are a few dressing rooms for the actors. Comfortable, but small, they are shelters from the frenzied activity. The leading players usually have luxurious trailers parked adjacent to the stage. Makeup tables sit near the dressing rooms. In some cases you'll go to the makeup building for your first makeup job, and then someone will do touch-ups on the set. The number of makeup people depends on how many actors are on call that day. If there are a lot, and the producer wants to save money, you can be sure that your morning call will be very early so that one makeup person can do several people.

So there you are at 7:00 A.M., made up and ready to go, except the schedule says that your scene is at 11:00 A.M. You know your lines—boy, do you know your lines—and now you try to stop going over them for fear you'll be stale by the time you say them. You contemplate a catnap, but that might take the edge off. Besides, you can't sleep. You can't take a walk because the schedule might change.

They begin shooting another scene at 9:00 A.M. It's a scene that appears much later in the script. As you watch, you become aware that the scene involves a character who's in your scene later on, and you start to form notions about that character regarding your scene. You then realize these notions are turning into strong ideas, and you begin to picture your scene in your head.

One word: LEAVE! Don't watch. You must only be concerned with how the other character relates to you in the scene you will be doing. The fact that movies are shot out of sequence can lead you to form opinions that are not valid.

The champion of champions in the "hurry up and wait game," is movie making. And you have to learn to play that game. My best suggestion is to do something that occupies your mind in a lighthearted way. Read an easy-to-read nonfiction book. Do a crossword puzzle. Play solitaire. Redo your address book. Exercise (without sweating). If you feel it necessary, do all of these things in character. The main thing is to keep your energy flowing, but not get involved.

There are some actors who don't need any of this. Anthony Hopkins, who played the maniacal Dr. Lector in *The Silence of the Lambs*, remarked that he was quite able to relax on the set, talk with friends and generally have a good time, and then, when it came time to shoot, immediately jump into character. On the other hand, Jodie Foster, also starring in the film, would do none of that. She was reportedly intense on the set and kept to herself between takes. That may or may not be true, but it illustrates a point. Very few actors can turn character on and off at will; jumping from laughs and jokes with friends to performing a serious dramatic scene.

Let's assume that you are one of those actors who wishes to focus on your work without too many distractions. You've kept active during your wait as suggested, and now they call you to the set. After greetings, the director asks to run the scene. Being the fine actor you are, you listen carefully to the other character and respond accordingly. After a couple of suggestions, the director blocks the scene very loosely. You can be sure the director has the blocking already in mind, because the set is lit and the camera is placed. Still, you're allowed some creative latitude, and if you can't do a move gracefully, chances are the director will change it.

At this point, most likely the director of photography (DP) will want to do some last minute tweaks and will ask you to stand in various key spots so that work can be done. The DP may carry a light meter, a small black object, and hold it very close to your face. On an efficient set, this last-minute tweaking of the lighting shouldn't take long, and the assistant director (AD) will then call for silence and say something like, "We're going for a take!"

If you're normal, your adrenaline will start to boil. The director calls for one last rehearsal and makes minor adjustments, which can range from a simple reminder to the camera person regarding a move to, in rare cases, a complete redo of the blocking and the performance.

It is the latter decision that concerns us. I am assuming that at this point you have not done 15 movies, but even if you have, you should still remember this next sentence: *IT IS NOT YOUR FAULT.*

Actors tend to become paranoid when a scene doesn't work for the director. But try to think of this—maybe it just doesn't work, and no one is to blame. Keep still, keep quiet, and wait. It may be a move. It may be a line. Wait for the fix to emanate from the director.

A good director usually will huddle with the actors and solicit their opinions. Now, you may speak if you wish. I've observed scenes become entirely different by the simple direction of one actor doing, or not doing, a piece of business, or looking away or not looking away, at a given time. Whatever you do, don't make radical changes on your own. You will have a tendency to try harder. Don't!

The same paranoia also develops when there are multiple takes. Never ask the director if it's your fault. There can be so many reasons for multiple takes, they're impossible to list. But when this happens, the thing you can do as an actor is to make subtle changes in the delivery. I emphasize the word *subtle*. This will happen naturally if you are listening and reacting to the other character. Remember, it is the action that needs to be repeated as near the same as possible on each take, not the acting.

To do the exact same performance time after time reduces you to being a puppet, not to mention a very dull actor. You should repeat exactly only when the director requests it.

You should look upon the set as a friendly environment. In an interview, Robert Mitchum remarked that he had just acted in a picture with a young actress who was quite nervous. Mitchum pointed out to her that the entire crew was on her side, pulling for her. Unless you go out of your way to earn their animosity, this is quite true. Allow yourself to feel this support. A film crew is one of the most highly skilled groups of people you'll ever meet. The craft demands technical perfection, and all of their skills are dedicated to making the actors look and sound good. Think about it—they wouldn't be there if it weren't for the actors.

The Location

A location shoot is exactly what the name suggests. You go someplace away from the studio to make the film or some scenes in it. The same studio rules apply to a location shoot with just a couple of exceptions.

First, if the location is a public place, where people from the area are allowed to watch, the actor must be wary of playing the goodwill ambassador to the detriment of the job. This is especially true on locations away from the environs of Los Angeles or New York, anyplace where films are not usually shot. The distractions can be enormous. The urge to respond to the locals' natural curiosity is insistent. They'll stare, shout, and ask for autographs. It doesn't matter if you have a tiny, tiny part. The fact that you're there with the movie company makes you a celebrity.

What do you do?

You've been raised to be polite.

These people buy the tickets. They're your audience. The fact is, you don't really have to do anything. When a film goes on location, someone is usually appointed to take care of these situations, a location publicist, the production manager, or even an assistant director. The point is, you don't have any responsibility to respond actively.

The best way to deal with the local watchers is to manufacture a wonderful smile. You put it on when you leave the dressing room, and you lose it when you reach the camera. You don't listen to what they say, nor do you answer. Your smile is enough. I might add that sometimes you'll hear a few unflattering remarks regarding your anatomy or your family tree. These especially should be ignored. Smile. The funniest question, which I've heard many times, is "Who are you?" This one, for sure, doesn't deserve an answer.

The only other location danger has to do with your fellow workers. There is a real bonding on location, a true sense of family and good feelings. The one important thing to keep in mind is that no one cares what the crew looks like the next day. They are not on camera. You are.

It's easy to get caught up in the fun after a hard, long day of shooting. But the makeup person can only do so much, and those closeups can be deadly.

Another note about makeup. Do not "improve" the makeup person's work. Makeup people know what they're doing, and you don't. If, by chance, you're on a really low-budget shoot or a student film where there is no makeup person, remember one thing—stage makeup technique looks grotesque on camera. Women should make up for everyday life, the time of day being important. Your eyes should look natural and your foundation not too pale. Avoid severe lines and shadows.

Men with ruddy skin tones usually don't need any makeup. The others just need a base to warm up the complexion. Avoid any eye treatment that one can see. In other words, if you look made up, the camera will see it.

Lights, Camera, Action

Good film and television actors must always know where the camera is, but never show it. They should also know where the key lights are and the microphone. The idea that the technicians will catch you no matter where you go, what you do, and how softly you whisper is a conceit. Norman

Jewison spoke of a very famous actor who purposely did the scene differently on each take. He never bothered to try to match the action. In fact, he went so far as to introduce new business when they shot coverage. As a consequence, in the editing process they had very little to choose from, because nothing matched. The actor's performance, as good as he is, was limited by his perversity on the set.

The key light catches the actor's expression and is an essential tool of the cinematographer. If you have a small part and, in the course of the scene, park yourself in front of the star so that your shadow prevents the key light from hitting her, chances are you're going to hear, "Cut!" Several keylights are placed strategically on the set to catch various moments in the scene. A quick glance during rehearsal will tell you how to clear those lights. Now, there are occasions when the set is lit without keys. You can usually identify this situation by seeing that the lights are not shining directly onto the set, but rather are bounced off white cards. Another way of getting this soft light effect is to put diffusion in front of the lamps. Sets or locations lit this way eliminate shadows to a great degree and thus make it easier for the actors to stay out of each other's light.

You may well ask why the actor should worry about such things. The answer is not to worry. Assess the situation, put it in the back of your mind, and then act. A good director and DP watch for any problems in rehearsal and modify either the lights or the blocking to correct them.

What you will normally hear after someone yells "Quiet on the set!" is this. A loud bell tells people outside the set that a take is being shot. Then the assistant director says, "We're going for a take. Roll sound."

SOUND PERSON: "Sound rolling."
ASSISTANT DIRECTOR: "Roll camera."
CAMERA PERSON: "Camera rolling."
SOUND PERSON: "Speed."
ASSISTANT DIRECTOR: "Mark it."
SLATE PERSON: "Scene 32 'Apple' Take One."

And then the person holding the clapboard clicks it shut and leaves. The director then says, "Action!" There may be one slight change. The clapboard person may not say the scene number and just click the board shut. This is because the sound person has already slated the scene at the recorder stand. Don't say any lines until the director says "Action!" or whatever, but while all of this is happening, get into the scene. Establish eye contact with the persons you're doing the scene with, and think of what you'll be saying when the scene starts.

When the scene is finished, the director says, "Cut!" Now this is very important. Do not stop acting the second you hear "Cut!" A good camera operator will continue to roll for 5 or 10 seconds after he hears "Cut!" Some of the best reactions happen during those seconds. Wait until the set begins to stir and you sense that indeed the camera is off.

Starting and stopping the camera wastes film. Once the actor understands this and behaves correctly, the producer will be a happy person. To illustrate: You are in closeup for two or three lines. You blow it. You're embarrassed and angry with yourself. Don't move away and leave the scene. Forget it immediately.

Stay in character and start again. One more goof? It's OK. Begin again. You can do three or four takes in this fashion and still use less film than if you had stopped and lost position, thus forcing a camera stop. The director may even give you direction while the camera rolls. The camera operator may ask you to tilt your head 2 or 3 inches. The important thing is to keep working in character. Even your expression when you blow your lines, if it's in character, can be used.

The standard procedure is to shoot a master and then shoot coverage—the closeups. This usually means the set needs some preparation and lights need to be moved, which can take from 10 minutes to half an hour or even more. Your task is to remember which take or takes the director chose to be printed and what your performance was on those takes.

A brief technical note—on multiple takes, the director will make a decision to print one, two, or maybe three versions. Because printing the film is expensive, they make this limited selection so they can watch the chosen takes the next day. This viewing is called *watching the dailies*.

On budget-minded television movies, the director tries to limit the number of takes to one or two. In this case they'll usually print both of them.

Back to your coverage. The setup is completed, and you are ready to do the scene again, this time in closeup. Again you are allowed to make subtle changes. But this time, with the camera so close, you must be wary of making large moves. After your coverage, the camera is reversed, and you do the scene once again for the other actor's closeup.

Say this is the only scene scheduled for you today, and the call sheet says your other scene is tomorrow. The crew is setting up on another set.

Do not leave.

Do not get out of costume.

Go to your dressing room and wait. Either the assistant director or a production assistant (P.A.) will come and release you. The P.A. will also remind you of your next call and confirm that you understand. By the way, during the work day, whenever you leave the set, no matter how short a time, you always tell the A.D. or P.A. exactly where you're going.

Sound

Modern technology has given the sound person many new tools to capture what the actors say. These very sensitive instruments also record every other sound on the set, so the actor must be extra careful not to handle props in a way that would cover dialogue. The keys you put on the table make quite a racket. If there is no dialogue at that time, the sound editor can soften that racket very easily, but if you happen to talk as you put the keys down, you may just cover the line so that it is unusable. Chairs squeak. Newspapers rustle. Ice cubes in glasses rattle.

You must be aware of these noises and do your best to speak around them. The fact that they seem to you to make hardly any noise is deceiving, because the microphone amplifies sound.

In a scene between two actors, the sound person usually uses one microphone. The boom person holds the mike on a large pole and switches it back and forth as each actor speaks. The use of one mike means that both voices are being recorded on one channel. Therefore, if one actor speaks in whispers and the other in normal voice, it is necessary for the sound mixer to adjust the volume quickly so each is recorded at nearly the same leve.. The aware actor tries to match the volume of the other actor doing the scene. There's some license in this, so you don't have to worry about being absolutely accurate. It is only when the difference is extreme that insoluble sound problems occur, and it becomes necessary for the actor to loop.

ADR: Looping

Automatic Dialogue Replacement (ADR or *looping*) is a method of recording lines of dialogue that for technical reasons could not be done while shooting. Looping is also used when the director is not satisfied with a line reading and wishes to get another interpretation.

Because so many films nowadays are shot on location, looping has become a major part of production. Bob Baron, the ADR mixer at Paramount Pictures, estimates that between 40 to 90 percent of dialogue is looped. In an interview, Baron gave me the following tips for the actor.

ADR stages are recording studios, usually sterile environments with a very dead sound. The microphones are set up in front of a large movie screen. The film is cut so the actor sees only that portion he is to work on. This is usually one or two lines at a time.

Sound technicians play back the lines to be replaced so you can get an idea of the rhythm. Listen carefully. Then on the next rehearsal, mouth the lines while listening to yourself on the screen. At this point, the director may make suggestons for interpretation, and the mixer will ask for a voice check.

There are times on a set when you do your lines without the words being recorded. This is called MOS, which when translated means Mit Out Sound. This odd phrase came about years ago when a German director, who couldn't pronounce *with*, used the German word *mit* instead to call for takes without sound. Back to ADR.

When it's time for a take, the picture comes on the screen, usually a few seconds before your line. Then you'll hear three quick beeps just before you are to speak. These beeps are rhythmically placed. Feel the rhythm, and begin your dialogue when the logical fourth beep would come. On paper it would appear:

Beep . . . Beep . . . Beep . . .
DIALOGUE

The most common mistake is to come in too soon after the third beep. Think of the beeps as a musical introduction.

The sound track has been cleared of all extraneous sounds so that your voice is the only thing you hear (unless another actor has an interjection). Because of this, you'll feel quite naked, and your tendency is to pull back. Don't. If anything, the mixer wants more voice, more emotion.

Quite a bit of ADR takes place because of shooting at noisy exteriors. Cars honking, planes overhead, a city bus at the corner, all conspire to bury your lines. Now when you listen to the track, you'll not hear any of this general noise. It will be added later. But you must remember that it exists when you redo your lines, so use more breath and more volume than you think you need, because when you played the scene on the street you heard the clamor and tried to rise above it.

Even if you're in the distance, keep the level up. The mixer can create the right perspectives when all of the elements are there in the final mix. If you try to create that perspective as you record, you make it more difficult.

Most actors agree that laughing and crying are the most difficult looping assignments. There you are on a modern sound stage watching something you did perhaps a month ago, and the person on the screen—you—is physically carrying on, either laughing hysterically or sobbing your heart out. On the sound stage, there's no other actor to play against, and you have to recapture the mood. It's like being at a party and having someone say, "Be funny," or "act."

Yes, it's difficult, and a lot of actors hate it. But it is a necessary ingredient in the process and must be done. If you accept this and understand the technical process, ADR can be a very creative process. Most important for the actor is to realize that all of the other elements, ambient sound, music, and so on, will be added later. You should keep that in mind for your performance. That naked solo voice you hear now is not the way the film will sound.

An excellent way to practice ADR is to lip-sync a song. Learn one of your favorite songs and tape yourself lip-syncing it making *no* sound. Then, on playback, sing along with your image, trying to match your voice to your lips. Play it back while someone videotapes you singing along. It would be wise to pick a song that makes more use of the language than "oh, oh baby."

Outside Elements

Movie sets and locations attract a lot of activity. Publicity people bring in the press for interviews. The front office has a tour for money people, or VIPs. The various actors' agents show up. Friends and relatives gawk from the perimeter. During the breaks, people eat, talk, conduct other business, and tell jokes.

It is not a serene environment. If you wish serenity, make your spot inviolate. If you have a dressing room, go there. If not, do the best you can. Making a movie involves a lot of people doing a lot of jobs. Accept that, and you'll be happy. The fact that you have to cry your heart out in 10 minutes because in the script your dog was killed and it's near the end of the day and you know you're not going to get more than two takes doesn't make a bit of difference. Just do it!

11

Scenes

Numerous books with scenes from plays and movies are available. For this book, with a couple of exceptions, I have used only original material I wrote especially for students so that you can't compare yourself with the performer who created the role. In a couple of my acting/directing classes where we used scenes from produced movies, one woman would study the movie scene so thoroughly that she would always bring in a carbon-copy performance. When I asked her not to do this, she replied that the actresses she copied were so much better than she. Her theory was to emulate them on the chance that something would rub off in the process.

Acting, as you know by now, has nothing to do with that kind of imitation. So to prevent such copying, I have written original scenes. The literary merit of the material doesn't matter, and the fact that you don't know how each scene fits into a larger whole is also irrelevant. Make the scene a world unto itself. I hope the material suggests specific conflicts, subtexts, and goals. But you should feel free to extend, change, and invent, with only one admonition: don't change the dialogue.

EXERCISE 25: THE LANGUAGE BARRIER

ONE doesn't speak English. He/she has been sent to an office. TWO greets ONE as he/she enters.

TWO

Hi . . . I'll be with you in a
minute.

Two completes some work while One smiles and waits. After a bit, Two approaches.

TWO

Have you come about the job?

One hands Two a piece of paper. Two reads.

                TWO
You don't speak much English.

                ONE
Yes.

                TWO
You *do* speak English?

                ONE
Yes.

                TWO
Well that's good . . . What
about word processing?

                ONE
Yes.

                TWO
Excellent. The job requires a
lot of word processing. Are you
familiar with MicroSoft Word?

                ONE
Yes.

                TWO
Which version?

                ONE
Yes.

                TWO
Excuse me?

                ONE
Yes.

                TWO
Uh . . . Are you Stalin's ille-
gitimate heir?

                    ONE
Yes.

                    TWO
Do you know any other words in
English?

                ONE/TWO
                (TOGETHER)
Yes.

Two now speaks slowly and louder as if that would
help the person understand.

                    TWO
This job requires someone who
speaks English . . . English! You
don't speak English. No . . .
speak . . . English . . .

One smiles at Two.

                    TWO
NO ENGLISH!

                    ONE
Yes!

                    TWO
Not yes . . . NO.

                    ONE
Yes.

                    TWO
NO! . . . . NO! NO! NO!

                    ONE
No?

Two is relieved and hands the paper back.

                    TWO
Good-bye and good luck. I have a
lot of work to do . . . so thank
you.

One hands Two the paper again.

                    TWO
          No . . . you take.

Two tries to hand it back, but One refuses to take
it.

                    TWO
          You take! Please . . .

Two struggles to get it back into One's hand.

                    TWO
          This is exhausting.

Finally One takes the paper and gestures for Two to
read it. Two tries to comprehend.

                    TWO
          Look . . . The job requires . . .
          Why am I saying this?

                    ONE
          Macka . . . Macka.

One puts his/her arms around Two's neck and pulls it
to the paper.

                    TWO
          I'm going to have to call some-
          one.

                    ONE
          Macka!

One gestures from their eyes to the paper.

                    TWO
          Macka? What? Read?

Two begins to read the paper and suddenly stops,
looks at One, then back to the paper. One lets go as
Two straightens up to read. The paper slowly comes
down as Two looks intently at One. One realizes that
Two is understanding. Two goes to the desk, takes

```
out an old milk carton, then comes back to One. Two
looks at the picture on the carton, than at One.
```

                    TWO
          Sister/Brother!

```
They embrace.
```

                                        END OF SCENE

Yes, I know, One has all of the good lines. The scene relies on the sincerity of One and the polite frustration of Two. At the end, at the moment of realization before Two goes to get the milk carton, the scene can be played most seriously. This sets up the payoff.

The business with the paper and One's physical move compelling Two to read it must be carefully worked out. The neck business should not be too aggressive—annoying but not alarming. Passing the paper back and forth should also be choreographed so it happens on certain lines each time.

EXERCISE 26: COLLEGE BOYS

One and Two are roommates. They have just come back from summer break and each is unpacking his things. Once again, the business must create a pattern, and you must adhere to it on each take. The actors should inventory the items in their suitcases or duffle bags and know the order and where they go.

                    ONE
          So . . . how did it go?

                    TWO
          Great.

                    ONE
          I had to work for my Dad for
          three weeks, but then I went to
          New York for a week.

                    TWO
          You didn't even call.

                    ONE
          I did too. They said you were in
          Kansas.

TWO

Oh yeah . . . that was the week
my Grandfather died. Damn, I
wish I'd been there. I could
have showed you around.

ONE

It would have been nice.

TWO

So what did you do, besides
getting drunk?

ONE

Things.

TWO

Things? You act like you get to
New York every month. So what
did you do? Visit the Empire
State? The Statue of Liberty?

ONE

I went to the Guggenheim Art
Museum.

TWO

What?

ONE

And I went to see a symphony
concert.

TWO

You went to a symphony concert?

ONE

I was going to go to the opera,
but they were shut down.

TWO

They do shut down in August.

ONE

So instead we went to see a
play.

                    TWO
We? Did I hear you say we?

                    ONE
Oh . . . didn't I tell you? I
met someone.

                    TWO
You didn't just meet someone.
You met a sorceress . . . maybe
a witch.

                    ONE

Look out!

                    TWO
You're the one who should look-
out. Art museums . . . symphonies . . . Man, you have been
transformed . . . Mutated!

                    ONE
What are you getting so excited
about? You been trying to get me
to do that stuff for two years.

                    TWO
You're right. Guess I wasn't
pretty enough . . .

                    ONE
That's for sure . . . So . . .
what about you?

                    TWO
Me? I just wasted my time going
to museums, symphonies . . .
plays . . . same old shit . . .
except, I met someone too.

                    ONE
That's great.

                    TWO
Remember Harold from down the
hall?

                    ONE
Yeah.

                    TWO
He was always bragging about his
sister.

                    ONE
Eunice.

                    TWO
Hey, you remembered her name.
I'm amazed.

                    ONE
I'm afraid you will be.

                    TWO
What makes you say that?

Two begins to put it together. They each reach into
their cases and pull out a framed portrait of
Eunice.

                ONE/TWO
We're engaged.

                                    END OF SCENE
_____

EXERCISE 27: TWO WOMEN

                    TWO
I told him that I had decided to
become celibate.

                    ONE
What did he say?

                    TWO
He asked me what I meant by
that. I explained it to him.

                    ONE
And he took it like a man.

                    TWO
In a way. He said we should have
one for the road.

                    ONE
You were in the car again?

                    TWO
It's an expression. Remember the
song that old guy used to sing?

                    ONE
Julio something or other?

                    TWO
No . . . An American. Anyway I
said no.

                    ONE
You're a very principled woman.

                    TWO
I want an uncluttered life with
uncluttered relationships where
I know that I am liked or dis-
liked for what I am. Besides, I
think I'll have more time to
study.

                    ONE
You'll get straight As and be a
nervous wreck. Personally, I'll
settle for C-plusses, if you get
what I mean.

                    TWO
I didn't expect you to do it
just because I did.

                    ONE
What a relief.

                    TWO
I know it's an important means
of expression for you.

ONE

It makes me want to sing and tap
dance . . . What do you mean, an
important means of expression?

TWO

It fulfills you.

ONE

How do you know what it does to
me?

TWO

You told me so.

ONE

I have never said that word
fulfill in my life. You know
what you're fulfill of.

TWO

I knew if I told you, that you'd
have some sort of jealous fit.

ONE

Jealous of what? Some twit who's
had three . . . no, make that
two and a half, ten-second bouts
in the back seat of a Toyota
with a man who doesn't know the
meaning of celibate.

TWO

It was a full three.

ONE

You said somebody walked by.

TWO

They did . . . but it was
consumated.

ONE

Consumated? You've been
consumated? I didn't know. You

```
                poor dear . . . No wonder you're
                giving it up.
```

One begins to laugh. Two doesn't want to, but she
soon joins in. They both ad lib with the word
consumated as a theme.

END OF SCENE

EXERCISE 28: MAN AND WOMAN

This scene without obvious content is an acting challenge. The words are
not at all what the scene is about. Create your own subtext, do the scene, and
then upon viewing, ask the group what they thought it was. Did their views
match yours?

```
                        HE
        Hi.

                        SHE
        Hi.

                        HE
        Did you have a good time?

                        SHE
        Not really.

                        HE
        Where's your coat?

                        SHE
        I didn't take one.

                        HE
        I could have sworn you took a
        coat.

                        SHE
        I didn't need it.

                        HE
        Weren't you cold?
```

                         SHE
No . . . Well, the air condi-
tioning was a bit chilly.

                         HE
It isn't air conditioned.

                         SHE
It most certainly is.

                         HE
That must be new.

                         SHE
It was there from the start.

                         HE
They never used it when I was
there.

                         SHE
Perhaps you were there in the
winter?

                         HE
It was spring . . . I was there
once in June . . . But it was a
cold damp June.

                         SHE
They often are.

                         HE
Yes.

                         SHE
Not like now.

                         HE
So you wished you had taken your
coat?

                         SHE
I suppose.

                         HE
It always seems that when you
take your coat, you never need
it. Then, when you take it, it's
. . .

                         SHE
Hot.

                         HE
Yeah.

                         SHE
I don't think you should say
that's always true.

                         HE
I didn't mean always.

                         SHE
That's what you said.

                         HE
People always say always, but
they really don't mean it.

                         SHE
I don't. I mean I don't say
always.

                         HE
O.K. You don't.

                         SHE
When I say always, I mean it.
That's why you'll seldom hear me
say always.

                         HE
You don't like . . . small talk.

                         SHE
No.

                         HE
I could tell.

                    SHE
        I suppose.

                    HE
        No supposing about it.

A long pause.

                    SHE
        It was damn cold in there.

                                    END OF SCENE
_____

   You might experiment with this scene by choosing a specific locale, situation or costume, then make a drastic change of these elements on a second take.

_____

EXERCISE 29: THE COMEDY SKETCH: CASA BLANCO

Ext: Airport
Bogart and Bergman, AKA Ricky and Ilsa, are about to
say good-bye in the moody mist. Ricky is world
weary, tough and taciturn. Ilsa, has the accent of a
Maitre'D in a bad continental restaurant.

                    RICKY
        O.K. baby, you're getting on
        that plane and that's that.

                    ILSA
        Oh, Wicky, Wicky, Wicky.

                    RICKY
        That's Ricky, Ricky, Ricky.

                    ILSA
        I just said that.

                    RICKY
        You said, Wicky, Wicky, Wicky

                    ILSA
        Wight!

RICKY

Wong . . . I mean wrong! It's
Ricky with an R. Not Wicky with
a W!

ILSA

Honey, don't be angwy. I want to
stay with you. I love you.

RICKY

Your place is with your husband.
He needs you.

ILSA

I don't love Wictor.

RICKY

That's Victor!

ILSA

Wight! Why do you repeat evewy
thing I say?

RICKY

Forget it.

ILSA

This may be the last time we see
each other.

RICKY

I know . . . But we have our
memories and our special song.
(hums tuneless melody)
Da dee da da dee da

ILSA

What's Da dee da da dee da?

RICKY

I forgot the words.

ILSA

You forgot the tune . . . You
forgot the words to our song?
How could you do such a thing?

Rick continues to sing the same two lines over, trying to remember. She continues on through this and he sings louder.

>   ILSA
> You swore you'd never forget it.
> You sang it to me after we made
> love the first time. We danced
> to it on the night we parted.
> You made a hit record of it!
> WILL YOU SHUT UP?

>   RICK
> I think I've got it! (sings)
> Twinkle Twinkle little . . .
> Little . . .

>   ILSA
> Little jerk.

We hear the roar of the airplane engine.

>   ILSA
> Thank goodness.

>   PA VOICE
> Flight 202 leaving for Lisbon.

>   RICKY
> This is it baby.

>   ILSA
> Take singing lessons while I'm
> gone. And maybe a memowy course.

>   RICKY
> What's a memowy course?

>   ILSA
> Forget it . . . . Maybe you're
> wight. Wictor needs me. Fwance
> needs me. Good-bye Wicky.

She kisses him on the cheek and leaves.

                         RICKY
              That's Ricky. (to himself)
              What's that dumb song.

                        PA VOICE
                         (SINGS)
              Twinkle Twinkle little star.

     Rick reacts.

                    RICK AND PA VOICE
                         (SINGS)
              How I wonder what you are.

                         RICK
              Here's looking at you kid!

END OF SCENE

If several couples do this scene, it would be best to tape it without an audience. Also, withhold playback until all of the versions have been taped. The jokes will get stale, but you should overlook that and watch for technique. Once again, the actors must play it straight and let the humor evolve from characterization. Don't play to the jokes.

EXERCISE 30: DISCOVERY

    You are looking for a book. You find one and sit
    down to read. A letter drops from the book and you
    silently read it. *Write this letter before perform-*
    ing the scene. What does the letter say? After
    playback, ask the group for their interpretation.
    Then read the letter aloud.

END OF SCENE

For further study, I would take scenes from plays rather than films and tape them utilizing film techniques.

With respect to the authors and only for the purpose of exercise you should cut the dialogue to a minimum. In other words, make them more like film scenes.

12

The Business

Film and television production costs money, lots of money. It is not a misnomer when they call it the motion picture industry. On one side you have the creative elements and on the other, the business people. In between lies a small battleground. I say small because there is an awareness on both sides of what the problems are and an accommodation because of them.

The actor plays an important role in this real-life drama. Those who write about the excesses of the movie business usually point the finger at directors. But actors have their parts also. It is a small community and one can get an unsavory reputation in it very quickly.

Critics of actors usually mention one or all of these faults: 1. unprepared; 2. incompetent; 3. difficult. Actors should be especially wary of being labelled difficult. A movie production is a complex organization where many skilled and creative people deal with both high technology and artistic expression. It is an ideal spot for Murphy's Law; which says that when things are going wrong, they'll get worse. Through no fault of yours, you are thrust on a set where Murphy's Law has struck with a vengeance. You finally get to do your four lines and you are great. Then a small voice announces that the camera jammed and none of it was usable. They then announce lunch and you have to wait.

After lunch, you prepare to redo the scene, but the producer insists the lines aren't right. The director and producer now huddle together, each throwing lines to try and fix the scene. The result is a hodgepodge of what you did before, without the finesse.

You work on the new lines, and it's time for a take. Halfway through, the director yells, "Cut!" and huddles with the producer, and you feel their eyes on you. You know they're thinking it isn't the dialogue, it's the actor. But you're wrong. Another change, a brief rehearsal, and they're ready to shoot again. You get a lot of encouragement and praise and are ready to emote. Halfway through, a large jet flies over at 400 feet.

Let's face it. You have every right to be thoroughly upset. As Archie Bunker would say on "All In the Family," *"Stifle it!"*

If you expect and prepare for Murphy's Law, you can face these difficulties with equanimity. If you add to the chaos by making a scene, it will be duly noted, and even though the circumstances warranted some reaction, all that people will remember is your outburst.

Other actors who get called difficult are those who are never satisfied with their performances and insist on doing more takes. You can politely ask for one more take every so often, but to insist on it, after the director wishes to move on, is a definite breach of professional etiquette.

By the way, Murphy's Law for actors has a special twist—nothing bad ever happens when you are mediocre. It's only when everything seems to click that things go wrong.

Agents

You can't get a job without an agent, and you can't get an agent without a job. You'll hear this Catch-22 situation all the time. The fact is, you *can* get an agent without a job, but it takes real work, persistence, and the proper materials. The Screen Actors Guild publishes a list of agents, as do several private companies. Some of them designate whether or not they will see new people.

The proper materials are: 1. A brief one-page resume that lists your educational and acting experience. Do not list extraneous jobs that have nothing to do with the business. 2. A couple of good head shots (photographs). If you submit a glamour-type shot, also include a simpler shot that just looks like you. Many times I have been handed photographs by actors who bore no resemblance to their much-glamorized pictures.

The hard work and persistence factors have to do with not being discouraged and keeping a positive attitude. You must know that someday, something will happen.

One of the better ways to get an agent is to join an actor's showcase, one of the studios where actors, for a fee, attend workshops and every so often do scenes for invited guests.

Join a little-theatre group. The important thing is to make as many contacts as you can. You never know where that tip about a job will come from.

Should you move to Los Angeles or New York? It depends on what you want. You would find many more opportunities to do stage work in and around New York, and you might want that extra year of honing your craft. On the other hand, Los Angeles offers the prospect of being discovered for movies or TV. Your first part could be a starring role. Either place is filled with people just like you, all looking for work.

My advice for the recent college graduate is to go somewhere and do regional theatre for a year or so. If there's a film school nearby, try to do student films and videos.

For employment, I suggest a job that offers time flexibility. Waiting on tables is a good example. It's easier to get someone to cover for you if an interview comes up than it might be if you had an office job. It seems as though half of the wait people in New York and in L.A. are actors.

Auditions and Casting

I asked Jane Feinberg, formerly a partner in Fenton and Feinberg, one of the best casting firms in Los Angeles, for her views on casting. The firm's credits include *Raiders of the Lost Ark*, *E.T.*, *Godfather II*, and *One Flew Over the Cuckoo's Nest*, among many other movies and television shows.

These are her remarks: "The producer hires a casting director during preproduction for her or his expertise in finding the right actors for all the parts in the film. Sometimes the project is already attached to a star, but when it isn't, the casting director formulates casting ideas from the stars down to the player who has one line. After reading the script, she makes a list of the parts and what types she believes should fill them. She discusses this list with the producer and the director, and after some consensus, proceeds to the next step.

She sends out sheets to agents telling them what types of actors the movie requires. The agents set up meetings with her for their clients, hoping to fulfill those requirements. The casting director meets those actors and chooses those who will then go on to meet and/or audition for the director and producer.

In general, this procedure is predicated on the fact that the actors have agents and are members of the Screen Actors Guild, known as SAG."

Now what about those actors without agents and no union membership? How do they get into this mechanism?

Besides casting specific projects, casting directors are also looking for fresh and interesting actors to add to their casting lists. They go to local plays, showcases, and workshops for that purpose. They also listen to friends who recommend people.

To meet these new actors, the casting director invites them to what is called a general interview. This is a very important meeting for the actor, and it has its dos and don'ts.

Because this meeting is non-specific, you just chat. You don't audition for a part. It is also difficult to explain. Why do two people like each other instantly, but two others don't? So there you are in this semi-spiritual nether land, hoping your two psyches meld.

Let's get to the *don'ts* and improve the odds.

Don't think you have to be charming, witty, blasé, worldly, diffident, sophisticated, smart, chic, flippant, rude, obsequious, smarmy, or cute.

Don't dress up or down; avoid wearing a bizarre creation from some weird designer, or the remnants of your sixties-looking wardrobe.

Don't bring in every picture taken of you since birth, or clippings showing each and every time your name has been in print.

Don't be late, make excuses, or take charge.

Don't lie.

Now for the *dos*.

Do be yourself!

Do give evidence of your training and your serious intent to be an actor.

Do be enthusiastic and focused.

Do, if you're asked to read a line for a small part, read it naturally and honestly. (**Don't** try to make this one line the summation of all your previous training.)

Do leave your picture, the one that looks like you, and a brief resume. On the resume, include only items that directly relate to acting. Hobbies like riding a bike or a horse are fine, but the fact that you have memorized all of the bird calls from Canada is irrelevant.

One last word on auditions. It's a horrible process on each side of the table. To make choices based on a five minute perusal of the script is impossible. Yet, you must do it. My best piece of advice is to pick out at least one speech, memorize it and look up from the page when you speak it. Give that line your best shot and hope that it coincides with the director's vision.

Unemployment and Rejection

If there is one word that would guarantee your success in this highly competitive business it is not talent or *luck*—it is *persistence*. An actor who sets goals and never stops working towards them almost always gets work. You cannot just wait around and hope something will happen.

Instead, you go to workshops, classes, and showcases, and read the trade papers and casting sheets. You work at conventions as a receptionist or hand out samples. You expand your social circles and purposely, without becoming obnoxious, let people know what you do—and want to do.

Better yet, have a rich relative who buys a studio. Lacking such a relative, find out if friends of friends, friends of relatives, old college pals of your father or mother, other contacts you can dredge up—have any connection whatsoever with the movie or TV business. Then look them up and let them know what you do. These may be long shots, but one could land you an acting job.

Harrison Ford was asked in an interview who discovered him. He replied, "I suppose if I had to say that someone discovered me, it would be a composer in Laguna Beach, Ian Bernard." The fact is that Harry Ford, as he was then known, was acting in a play that included music I had composed. I thought he was talented and sent him to meet a casting director I knew at Columbia Pictures. To tell you the truth, I had forgotten about it and was quite surprised when he mentioned it years later.

The fact is, you don't know where your break is coming from, so you'd better be ready, as you usually only get one. Stealing from the Boy Scouts, your acting motto should be—Be Prepared.

13

This Is a Wrap!

In the course of writing this book, I talked to a few actors and directors who said, "acting is acting," or "I just do what I do." These zen-like statements have little relevance to the student actor. In fact, they don't make sense. Very good actors would say this to me, and when I attempted to question them further, they would fall silent. I respect their feelings, but it made me wonder why they think that way.

I believe their words say something else about them. The fact is, they don't know what they do, and they don't care to examine the process in an intellectual manner. The muse is so fragile to them, they're afraid if they speak of technique, or even think about it, their creative juices will dry up. They're like the country guitar player who sets up the strings wrong and used weird fingering, but still plays incredibly well. He says, "Nobody learnt me different."

When I interviewed other actors, they thought about the question of stage versus film acting and, at first, denied any difference. But then, as questions arose, they realized there were many modifications in their techniques, almost commonsense modifications. When you know the sensitivity of a microphone, its ability to hear the slightest whisper, you are given a new acting tool. When you know the camera can focus in on your eyes to see the smallest tear, or hint of emotion, you realize how little you have to do to communicate.

Stage-trained actors with all of the basic tools should have no trouble with these modifications. Once they are aware of the possibilities of the camera, the perfection of technique should be easy. Not so the other way around.

Recently, a famous movie actress made her stage debut in a Broadway play. The critic for the *New York Times* suggested that the actress "internalized too much."

The word internalized could be a key to the difference between the two techniques. On stage, the audience is a participant in the process. The actor plays a certain way in response to that. You might say the actor reaches out to the audience. In film, the camera, an inanimate device, plays no part in the drama; the actor knows that feedback will come only from the director after the take. During the performance, it is only you, the other actors, and the camera. So, the camera goes to the actor. The good film actor realizes the closeup lens allows film actors to internalize with the knowledge that the camera will capture the most subtle nuance of their performance.

The actor who thinks the only difference between stage and film acting is making it smaller is missing opportunities to create a new technique. The actress who "internalized" too much for the stage is an excellent film performer, much in demand. In fact, she's a star. She is also proof that one can excel in film without stage training.

You may rely on your talent to surpass expectations, but you should rely on your technique to fulfill them.

I leave you with one thought about film and television acting: Nothing is forever. But once you've committed a performance to film, it will seem like it. Films you've long forgotten will show up as a video 5 years later and once again you'll be able to appraise your performance. Be gentle. Just think of how much you've improved since then.

Index